THE
SOUL PATH

Key Life Lessons

on

Living Consciously

Series "Key Life Lessons for Living your Higher Self"

Charol Messenger

THE SOUL PATH

Key Life Lessons on Living Consciously

Series "Key Life Lessons for Living your Higher Self"

Third Edition

ISBN-13: 978-1-7320717-1-1
Library of Congress Control Number: 2011914490

New cover art, book description, and author bio. Modified format. Vol. I rearranged, a little rewriting. Chapter titles further improved and more sections. Vol. II, part II rewritten and condensed.

Messenger Publishing

Denver, Colorado   charolmessenger.com   CharolM@aol.com

New cover art: "Spirit" by Bruce Rolff, ID 40981864, Shutterstock, standard license.

Best-selling author Charol Messenger is an honoree of Marquis Who's Who in America 2020. Her 15 book awards in nondenominational spirituality and personal growth include 5 international 1st Place and 2nd Place.

> I first talked to God when I was three years old, in my backyard, speaking up to the heavens. I remember a sunny day with clouds. *November 1975,* during a life-changing event, I saw the potential and true hearts of all humanity. The next day I began writing. *January 2019,* I was wakened by an inner nudging and Jesus began speaking to me the first Letter of many that he wishes to share with all humanity.

Reviews

"Enchanting journey of the inner self-discovery and healing."
– Michael Matik, London UK, Reiki Master

"Charol beautifully combines sharing higher-consciousness wisdom with her own experiences and practical recommendations, whilst also managing to peep into the future. Her ability to elevate readers' awareness, so that they can see their own soul path unfolding, truly shines in this book. Often, this journey will feel more and more familiar as readers absorb the revelations given in almost every step along the way. At some point an exciting realization starts to sink in ... that one will find out very soon what is waiting for them further down their soul path if they carry on. And what an amazing finding it is..."
~ **Remote Healer** under the guidance of Archangel Michael. Author of *Become Your Higher Self: Experience Fast Spiritual Awakening.*
becomehigherself.com michael@awakeningkey.com
Administrator of facebook.com/groups/becomehigherself

"The essence of one's development."
~ John S. Brennan, Founding Dean, Regis University School for Professional Studies, Denver, Colorado

"A timely guide to spiritual realization and practice ... especially the early stages. Emphasis on process, with stages easy to follow and relate to. Constantly inviting the reader to choose more, such as to choose one's true destiny. Suggested practices are practical with rich exhortations and questions. Loaded with cautions about false prophets and specific criteria on how to recognize true voices. Profoundly simple to read and reread as needed. An ongoing guide."

"*Masterfully written* 'handbook for the soul'."
~ Aurelia Tara, Reiki Master, Spiritual Teacher, Denver

"*The Soul Path* is truly inspirational! The content is passionately and beautifully written. It resonates within my heart and surely will resonate with all others who read it. I really find it to be inspired and brilliant! This 'how-to handbook for the soul' is a *masterfully written* practical guide for spiritual growth, a demonstration of the divine process of physical manifestation, a testimony to the love and grace ever ready to assist when our heart's desire is to serve Creator and Creation. I am most enthusiastic about the simplicity of the truth so eloquently expressed here. This book was truly a delight to read...." — Aurelia Tara, Reiki Master, Denver, CO

"We as humans find it hard to change, tenaciously holding onto our old ways. We know something is missing from our lives, but resent others telling us what we must do to find it. That is why *The Soul Path* works. Without preaching or belittling, it authoritatively lays out the way—complete with guideposts and cautions—to finding inner peace, leaving us emboldened and eager to embark on our own spiritual journey." — **Barbara Munson, co-author** of historical biography *Gilly: A Humble Crusader,* owner Munson Communications.

"This is a wonderful book, so full of knowledge and subtle teachings that I'll have to read it again and again to get the most out of it. Some of it is so familiar to my experience, some I haven't experienced yet but am looking forward to... I so much love the sweetness and generosity of the message... God's kindness does come through, on every page...." — **Jennifer, Denver CO**

"I felt a sense of the grandeur of the spiritual path, a sense of its rhythm and pace, and this was valuable to me as I am often impatient. I was better able to see the journey as an epic adventure rather than a means to an end." — **Reader, the Bronx, NY**

National Finalist USA Best Books
12 chapters published in *Pathways* magazine, Denver

"If the goal is noble, whether or not it is realized in our lifetime is largely irrelevant. What we must do, therefore, is to strive, persevere and never give up."

~ Dalai Lama IV

I first talked to God when I was three years old, in my backyard, speaking up to the heavens. I remember a sunny day with clouds.

November 2, 1975 at 2:00 a.m., Charol Messenger was shaken out of her mundane life during a sudden life-changing mystical event. After a harrowing week, turning to prayer for help, she fell into a deep slumber, in which she saw angels surrounding her amidst a heavenly glow, heard their chorus of song outside the Gates of Heaven, and felt the presence of Archangel Michael overlighting her. Throughout the night, revelations came in waves to Charol about humanity's future and she saw the potential and true hearts of all humanity. The next day she began writing.

January 13, 2019 3:30 a.m., Charol was wakened by an inner nudging and went to her meditation room. In the arm chair, while she was deep in the consciousness, Jesus began speaking to her the first Letter of many that he wishes to share with all humanity. Enveloped in his loving energy, feeling his grace and tenderness and inimitable Presence, she wrote down the words, and they were the first of many.

Contents

Introduction 1

Volume I
The Spiritual Life, *Now*

Part I: How to Be Fully Conscious and Aware

1. We Are Living in a Transformative Age of Change 7

2. Reaching the Sea of Bright Enthusiasm 9
    How to Release Regrets, Fears, and Disillusionment

3. How Self-Reliance Is Key to Attaining Higher Awareness 14

4. How Discerning Delusions and Grandiosity Can Prevent Personal
    Harm 17
    Discerning Stupendous Follies

5. How to Recognize Truth and Genuine Persons of Light vs. Cults,
    Liars and Charming Manipulators 22
    Seeing Beyond People's Facades

6. Our Resilience Sees Us Through It...27
    How to Survive the Challenges of the World

Part II: The Steps That Get You There

7. Ten New Universal Laws 33
    "Tenets of Clear Being"

8. How Being Aligned with Your Higher Consciousness Frees
    Your Optimism 38
    The Causes of Increased Intelligence

1. Respecting All

2. Selfless Service

3. Embracing Your Higher Calling

Conclusion

How Can You Know Your Soul Purpose?

9.   The Eight Petals of Self-Discovery 44

How We Blossom One Petal At a Time

1. You understand human frailty and accept it.

2. Divine wisdom fills your heart.

3. You unleash your inner power.

4. You undergo a radical alteration in your beliefs.

5. You awaken to your soul consciousness.

6. You enter the realm of universal teachings.

7. You embrace divine consciousness.

8. You fulfill your destiny.

10.   The Five Phases to Becoming Fully Higher Conscious and Being Whole 47

1. Expanding

2. Saturation

3. The "Second Awakening"

4. "The Return into the One"

5. Back in the World

Conclusion

Part III: Embracing Your Soul Self

11. The Key to Personal Certainty 55

12. How to Know Your Destiny 63

As you transform the inner, so the outer will transform.

13. How to Know When to Help Others 71

You need not change the world. You need only change yourself.

What does receiving the wise advice of your inner Self have to do with your present physical life? And how will it affect the way you live?

"The Separation from the Outer Mother"

Eight Criteria for How to Help Others

    1. Keep your heart open at all times.

    2. Smile, even when suffering.

    3. Live sweetness, honesty, and generosity.

    4. Lift their comprehension about their own suffering.

    5. Observe.

    6. Incite courage in others.

    7. Access, through centered clarity, the universal consciousness.

    8. Raise your vibration.

14. Exercise to Hearing the Inner Voice 76

15. Sources of the Divine Inner Voice 81

Your Higher Self

    First Stage of the Inner Voice Perception

Counselors of the Other Realms

    Second Stage of the Inner Voice Perception

Beginning to Serve Others

Third Stage of the Inner Voice Perception

Conclusion

16. Your Comprehension and Perceptions Expanding 98

17. The *Inner* World We Discover 104

Part IV: The Turning Point

18. Moving Beyond Your Past 109

    "The Turning Point"

19. Humanity's "Turning Point" 111

20. Our First Leap of Consciousness 114

    to Homo Sapiens

21. Humanity Is on the Brink 118

    Humanity's Awakening

Volume II
Your Personal Transformation

Part I

Invoking Your Serenity, Which Is Your Inner Strength 125

Your More Tolerant Self, This Is the Blessing 126

The Ageless Self 127

Your Presence in the World 128

Be Innovative 130

Aligning to Your Whole Self 131

Accepting the Divinity in Yourself 131

You As a Self Have Always Been 132

Your Transformation 133

Your Enhanced Self Begins Now 134

The Time for You Is Now 135

Part II

WE Are All an OCEAN of the Life Presence: One Being, One
Breath 139

You, Now 140

We Are the Society 141

How to Maintain Inner Stability 142

The Economy and How You Can Help Yourself 143

Tyrants and Bullies 146

Our Evolving Global Society.. 147

> 1. We are a people unparalleled to any age before us.
>
> 2. We who appreciate the human condition find ourselves in a world overpopulated and ill with a multitude of diseases.
>
> 3. New spiritual teachers of the planet carry an understanding of mind, heart, and being. They understand the levels of consciousness besides the physical.
>
> 4. The animal kingdom is also evolving in its level of consciousness.
>
> 5. While we may look elsewhere for our salvation, nevertheless the task of personal and social transformation is our own, individually.

Living As Your Intentional Self 151

Earth Is the *Result* of Our Reality 152

Through 2170... 154

Is Spirituality the Religion of the Future? 155

At the heart of all religions is a spiritual truth. Upon these truths may be rebuild together.

Evolving into a Higher Vibrational Being 160
    Exercise to Reconstitute Your Body and Consciousness into
    Your Higher Being

Appendices

The Messenger's Awakening 165

Vision 1 168

Vision 2 169

The Author... 172

More About the Messenger 174

The Messenger Books 177

Recommended Movies, Books, Audio, Video 179

Introduction

Volume I is the main body of *The Soul Path,* received through the Universal Consciousness during a period of exceptionally heightened awareness in 1994.

Volume II is supplementary essays, received 2011-2017, with insights on managing our personal transformation during humanity's transformation.

January 27, 2019

"Charol, it was me all along, from the beginning," Jesus told me, during meditation that day. "I am your Master Teacher. It's been me writing to you all these decades as the I AM and the Universal Consciousness. I've been behind everything you've been writing."

Volume I

The Spiritual Life, *Now*

Part I

How to Be Fully Conscious and Aware

1

We Are Living in a Transformative Age of Change

Do you live life spasmodically as if in the trenches of a war zone? Or are you tranquil and sensitive to the higher realms of perception?

If you enjoy life with a complete admiration for the possibilities that life offers, you are blessed and may not require any additional insights into how to completely relish who you are.

However, if you do not, most certainly the insights in these pages may be helpful to better understanding how to be at peace and happy, because such insights help us all to be more human. They help us to heal our sorrows and disturbances about living in a society that generally strangles our sense of wonder and bends our inner hope, as if to conquer our natural Self that is sweet and caring. Such insights teach us to surrender—to our inner light—all that troubles us, at least earnestly to devote ourselves to that potential.

The journey into self-realization is a sacred process of becoming soul-embodied. When we absorb spiritual insights as our style of being human, we touch the simplicity of our whole Self. When we commit in-depth to this process, we embrace our divine Self. While being human is not easy, we all can learn to understand the essential nature of life and how to live a blessed life . . . because soul actualized within us gives us that.

When traveling the ancient and well-worn inner path of awakening to our soul consciousness, we may be amazed at what we discover. We may cry. Undoubtedly we feel the sure connection of the Divine Presence within us . . . and we embrace that Presence as our essential Self. As we do, it is quite tremendous for us.

Personal happiness is possible during our current lifetime, says the Divine Mind, even with all the confusions that abound. When we are open to expanding in how we see our life and relationships, we become aware of the inner voice of reason prompting us with ideas of how to live a blessed existence; because when we are open in our personal experiences to our inner light, we touch our *godself*.

When we are guided by the inner light, nothing in society truly can bring us grief; because we are then embracing the full sweetness, honoring the complexities, and enduring the contrasts with tranquil patience and genuine compassion. We are opening our heart to the abundant joys of this world and the many peoples of many beliefs. We are surrendering our personal declarations to the philosophy, *"Live and let live."* We are so filled with appreciation that uncertainty and fear no longer overwhelm us.

When we absorb into the center of our being, our full, divine and eternal knowing Self, we are able to see all things just as they are, to see the vast untruths of this world and move through them wisely. We are able to focus on our strength and beauty and not be appalled by the restlessness of the many. Rather, we seek to help restore balance and to ensure safety and trust in all who struggle.

When we devote ourselves to living from our inner light—as well as we can, each day—we become one of those who is healing society. We do this with grace and real commitment; because when embodying the light of our soul, the wise Self we innately are, we are living wholeheartedly in every way.

With the counsel of the inner light of our soul, life is worth living. Catastrophes of what might be become sweet mysteries. Complexities become delightful puzzles to solve. We are so self-assured that life just works for us. That is the power of soul active in our lives.

So, with a deep appreciation for all that each of us innately is, let us now open the door to your soul awakening.

2

Reaching the Sea of Bright Enthusiasm

How to Release Regrets, Fears, and Disillusionment

For an aspirant on the soul path, life is fraught with unresolved desperations, because we are full from a life of anguish and wishful thinking. Even so, we are able to release all inhibiting quandaries, to reassess and recreate our incomplete dreams, to restructure and rebuild our hope. It is inevitable that one day we are so sure of ourselves, so determined, that all of our past conundrums fade away in a sea of bright enthusiasm.

When following the soul path, we awaken our inevitable Nature, which is both serene and dynamic. Our true nature is to be well and vital, without debilitating habits, reasonable yet challenging, believing in imagination and innovation, recognizing that we are wise and brilliant aspects of the illuminating presence of the Divine Intelligence.

When venturing upon the soul path, we self-evolve our entire personal philosophy, which requires a lot of us. However, we are powerfully able to redefine our human persona, to refine our need for exactness into a hopeful state of being, to restyle our habits that have been a false identity, to interact and treat ourselves from a natural expression rather than as a learned response based on the demands of our culture.

By engraving ourselves with new and more comprehensive ideals, we enable ourselves to be a great deal more satisfied with life. We eventually may even become a teacher to others who have not yet conceptualized *what can be*. This is a great reward for our effort.

When following the disciplines of the Universal Laws ("Tenets of Clear Being") because we prefer to be all we can be, we access our greater Self, our soul. Soul is our potential fully acted upon. Soul is our expanded understanding, comprehension, analysis, and reflection. When integrating our soul's consciousness in our behaviors, we are fully actualizing to our whole Self.

Soul does impose stringent applications that are challenging, because soul is that aspect of us that requires us to live with honor and devotion toward all of life. When beginning the soul journey toward our peaceful being, we come to recognize that our talents may be of benefit to all.

As we realize who we truly are and we no longer resist our unique Character, we pursue avenues of learning that will teach us various modalities and adages of the ancient wisdoms. As we embrace our courage, we hold fast to resourcefulness; we become incredibly alive in all that we do, and enthralled by the blessed presence of the Divine Consciousness that is working through us.

We are in life to expand our awareness and to explore awareness with others. The world is our stimulus for that. The world presents us with increasingly more complex lessons, through which we evaluate our choices and responses. When we view the world with an attitude of wonder and adventure, life becomes serendipitous opportunities. Life becomes more stable when we are more assured in our life experiences.

When embodying the attributes of our soul, it is easier to appreciate devotion to our various life tasks. We learn to love ourselves without judgment and to care for others without restriction. We learn to release expectations of others and to stabilize as our true Self.

Once we have let go of allowing our emotions and desires to control us, we are more than an aspirant on the soul path. We are an enlightened student of the ancient teachings of cosmic balance and goodwill. When prepared in our identity to take on the correspondence of our soul, we embark upon a new plateau, which endows us with the truer aspect of the divinity that is integrating within us.

As we awaken to our soul consciousness (higher consciousness), we *know* that the universal truths are constant in all realities and that those guidelines are eternal. We allow the principle forces of life to guide us toward a genuine affection of all peoples and a tolerance of all circumstances.

This is being divine. This is being our whole Self. Once we fathom this, we are beyond the perimeter of being an aspirant. We are training in the next degree of spiritual growth, of the several degrees that measure our progress in comprehending the values and aesthetic teachings of the spiritual wisdoms. Once we have imbued the *knowing,* we are reaching the highest aim toward which we have been evolving for all of our lifetimes.

When embarking upon the soul path, it is not the first time that we do so, although in the beginning we may not remember this. In fact, we are very familiar already with the soul path. We were born in soul.

Nevertheless, when resuming the soul path, until we have moved beyond the initial stages, we have yet to agree to live by the Universal Laws ("Tenets of Clear Being") and we are only curiously drawn to their concepts and ideals. At some point, however, it becomes quite clear to us that we are invoking a greater self-presence than we ever imagined we could. We begin to seriously analyze various avenues toward this abundant supply of what is the natural reality of the inner Self. Outer reality is tenuous. The inner dimension is free of inhibition and without conclusion.

When being our whole Personality, we are unafraid. We lack restriction in beliefs. We hold truth as a central value with which each person identifies. We know that truth is not an exterior form enforced by any outer law, but is a personal exhibition of universal principles that manifest through our natural identity . . . as a soul.

When embracing our soul's consciousness in our behaviors, we are on the path of healing our spiritual wounds. We are becoming focused and directed in pure thought, reason, and compassion toward all. We no longer dissuade ourselves. We no longer can conceptualize anything other than being whole.

By the time we incorporate our soul's wisdom in our mind, we are so imbued with our soul's point of view in our personality that our choices align with our highest level of being. We invoke the consciousness of the Divine as our model for living. We step into a commitment that, from that point forward, guides every aspect of our life. Our actions, words and thoughts—all choices that we make— become infused with the will of the Divine and we find that we can do nothing that is not in *that* accord. Once we infuse that Presence as our model for life, nothing else is real or even visible to us.

The blessed existence that is ours by universal privilege is already present in our being. The process of integrating our human personality with the Divine comes from healing our emotional pains and releasing our limiting thoughts and beliefs. . . until all that is left is the inner light we are, the state of consciousness of our unique and personal Self.

It is simple, says the Divine Mind:

> *Forgive. Release. Heal. The more you can forgive, the easier it is to be just who you are.*

We no longer live by expectations or demands. We live only to be our light, in all ways at all times available as a voice of compassion and inner truth . . . wherever Spirit moves us.

We are the Presence unfolding, peeling away our layers of unknowing, removing the veils that have clouded our true vision of life, dispelling disbeliefs that have clouded our passion, dissipating disillusionments that have saturated our vibration and made us sluggish with density, loosening and shedding our old skins of despair, discouragement, and discontent—until all that is left is the shimmering presence of our laughter, sweetness, devotion, and kindness. Until all that is left is our natural presence and expanding

Personality. We are filled to overflowing with the powers of life: consciousness, self-discipline, and a resonance with all. We overflow with the presence of the Divine, which radiates vibrantly through us, attuning us to every aspect of the web of creation. And we become this fabric, the living substance that binds every form of the great Mind of God.

Each of us carries this vision within. Whether we nurture this vision in ourselves is a personal choice. When seeking the path of truth and the wisdom of the ages, however, we cannot help but open our heart and mind to the inner world . . . wherein lies all knowing.

God, of which each of us is an aspect, is a living and vital Intelligence that permeates our very atoms. When we imbue the Divine Consciousness into our every thought, we evolve into our full and vibrant Self.

3

How Self-Reliance Is Key to Attaining Higher Awareness

In the pursuit of higher consciousness, we learn who we essentially are. This, in time, causatively affects our reality. We enhance our experiences and direct the way in which our emotions flow. When focused, this energy expands into all areas of our life.

For example, we learn to defend ourselves against the "mind-robbers," those who for their own purposes wish to direct how others live, such as through advertising, or propaganda: "Buy this. Buy this. Buy this.. Buy this idea." As we gain inner wisdom and inner strength, we are less affected or swayed by others' efforts to influence us. We are more self-directed and less motivated by what others want from us. We are less gullible, and also less despondent.

In the process of fulfilling our spiritual need, simultaneously we gain the maturity to be self-reliant. We learn about our talents, personal strengths, and particular qualities that bring others joy in our presence. Over time, as we heal our heart wounds—and forgive—we acquire peace of mind (accept our self as we are).

Exacting self-disciplines teach self-restraint, patience, and self-analysis. We learn to forgive and to be tolerant and sensitive. We gain insight into all circumstances that arise. We gain confidence, because it results from knowing our soul power and being in that power. We acquire empathy for the suffering of others and give all of ourselves toward being a *presence* of hope.

The promises of a spiritual life are to fully know ourselves, fully access our soul power, and fully be the creative individual we are. The process of becoming attuned to our soul is the process of healing our heart wounds.

By stabilizing emotionally, we become more resonant to ideas that are less obvious and more attuned to emotional variances in the world. By enhancing mentally, we conceptualize new thoughts, stretch our imagination, and endow ourselves with the intellect of the Ancients. The advantages are the abilities to analyze fairly and objectively, to dissect various parts of situations, to restructure and rearrange attitudes and proposed experiences, and to plan visually and coherently.

Mental clarity is a byproduct of spiritual oneness. Emotional harmony is a byproduct of alignment with our soul. Physical well-being is a byproduct of self-discipline, which is necessary for accessing the higher levels of consciousness. When aligned in our spiritual Self, we are a being of many aspects working together.

We attain self-mastery by first mastering the yens of our physical body, the urges of our emotional body, and the eccentricities of our mental body. When we seek to master any one of these, ultimately we will master all of them, says the Divine Mind. That is why to be truly spiritual, we must also be truly human.

When embracing our whole potential and living it fully each day, we are able to let go of everything in the world that is a temporary salve to the yearning of our heart for belonging. When living from our spirit, we are attuned to situations and people who will assist us in being our full and present Self. We are fashioning in ourselves a new image. We are seeing our true being. We are being courageous, forthright, and indispensable; serene and sweet, yet enduring and frank.

We learn to release all that does not inspire us or touch our heart. We learn to be a healer of others' pain, without making their pain our own. We learn to give without hurting ourselves. We learn to know when to give, to whom, and what to give. With the wisdom of our inner Self, we can be so aligned with the world that we see everything for just what it is.

The inner path is incredibly exciting. There is always a more grand moment just ahead. It is as if—for the first time—we are truly alive; as if, before, we were walking in a dream.

Physical life is not all there is. If we are not scaling our dreams and hopes and harnessing their potency, we are a shell of our true Self. If we are not emboldened by our soul's fire, we are a vague reflection of our true Self, a shadow when we could be a dynamic and powerful beacon. Physical life is important, yet it is only a part of what we are. We are so much more.

Life is much grander when we allow our spiritual Self the freedom to be all that we can be. Human beings are cosmic by nature. Our innate Character is a being of many aspects.

We are human—yet, more than this, we are sweet souls striving to flower.

4

How Discerning Delusions and Grandiosity Can Prevent Personal Harm

Discerning Stupendous Follies

To walk clearly in wisdom, walk with a discerning eye, acknowledge your inner knowing, and trust your senses of the obtuse. These are our innate God-given gifts.

Inner alignment is reached through cherishing what we seek to be. When we accept our inner certainty without resistance or fear, and we include others in our tranquility, we are able to step into the outer glamours and retain clear insight. From our inner vision, we are able to evaluate opportunities in their clear truth and to discern stupendous potential follies of apparent enormous successes as well as potential long-term gains or losses.

True personal power is attained by controlling our attitudes. We acquire true power by devoting our whole being to our most sacred longings. Power born in *right thought* lasts. The power we can depend upon is that which comes from our personal commitment to kindness and goodwill.

The power that does not control is the inner power, which is an innate sweet disposition. The power that does not destroy is the inner power, which is a blazing eternal flame of personal serenity.

When we live as our essential Self, our core Self—as honestly as we know how—everything we think and do pivots around that self-image. All of our choices and decisions pivot from a perception of what will bring us fulfilling and satisfying peace. We find ourselves able to discern which opportunities will burn out like the fuses of fourth-of-July firecrackers.

Opportunities may sparkle and appear to hold much glamour and promise, yet what are they really? What can we expect from them as they evolve? Will our later revelations be as delightful?

When living from the perspective of our essential Self, we are able to observe everything as if with an "eagle" eye. We have a long and wide vision. We are able to perceive all possible ramifications of our actions and able to envision all possible consequences of our decisions. In fact, we see the full spectrum of every choice before us.

Only when we do not acknowledge our inner truth, in every instance, are we following a path that may lead at best away from our heart's true desire, at worst to self-destruction. Only when we continuously deny our inner knowing and ignore our heart's desire are we seeding our own destruction, from which collapse is inevitable.

To achieve a full and joyful life—everyone's innate right—listen to and act upon what you *know* in your heart is your truth . . . and live that truth. All other aspects of your life will then manifest in all glory and gratification.

All that we desire begins by aligning our actions with our inner perspective. Self-persuasion leads only to collapse. When we measure our choices by our inner knowing, we find pathways opening abundantly, safely, and free of self-deception. When centered in our spiritual Self, we have self-esteem . . . and we choose wisely.

TV news often has people in anguish because many cultural beliefs are being destroyed. The sharp contrast between illusory fame and a person's true character is repeatedly being thrown into the light. We are continuously being forced to re-evaluate our own actions, by example of those in the limelight. In the news, we see that powerful persons who have been valued highly are able to fall from their positions of global recognition, or at least to be tainted. We realize that anyone who appears worthy actually may be deceitful or even destructive. Profound examples of delusion are being shattered. While this is healing in the long-run for society, the shock is personally painful.

Disappointment is painful. Yet such incidents reflect the nation's and the world's growth. When heroes fall from their pedestals, we grieve at their loss in our lives, because they are not the persons we believed they were. Each time such an event strikes the media, we are forced to re-evaluate our own actions, choices, and beliefs. We are also forced to decide whether we will forgive that individual for his or her human frailty. A bit of life experience does make us more forgiving, tolerant and understanding, even if we do not like what a person has done.

The fierce and quick laws of cosmic justice are piercing us all to our essential Nature, until we cannot avoid being forced to admit our duality. Society is being "drawn and quartered" by delusions of grandeur. We are being disenchanted by the "beautiful ones" to whom we have proffered our allegiance. We are repeatedly being amazed and disheartened at the frightful true behaviors of many leaders of social status who have succumbed to the delusion that they are above cosmic law; when, in fact, no one is. This is forcing us to admit the dichotomy that exists between our values and our lives. We are having to ask ourselves hard questions: Are we, also, vain and pompous in our seductions of others' praises? Or are we servants of goodwill?

None of us can continue to ignore our personal emptiness. We cannot continue to subjugate our precious correct insights. As long as we do, we are sucked into The Lie.

The solution is bringing more of our Nature into our behaviors, beliefs, and concepts of what is honorable and worthy. When we place our trust in ephemeral and fleeting outer purposes of superficial successes, we make ourselves vulnerable to the same strategic mistakes as we now observe in so many others.

To live in a peaceful world, we must build a peaceful heart, and only we know whether we are honoring our highest aspect or destroying it by repeatedly ignoring our own value.

This world of delusions is so familiar that we often do not see the truths behind the facades. We dance within our desires and avoid principles of kindness and goodwill.

The solution is to embrace the simple honesties that give us inner peace. With peace intact, all else that comes to us is a bonus.

Our pure Self dreams of surrendering to noble actions, dreams of sensitive reflections, embraces genteel perceptions, and is unable to fathom self-destroying behaviors. Such words and thoughts are impossible.

When we embrace our kind and lovely Self, we cannot also embrace our demanding and obnoxious self, because only one of these can be predominant in our psyche.

We live in an age of enormous duality. Society professes beliefs that we as individuals do not act upon. We act out what brings us temporary pleasure. We lose ourselves in the moment, rather than hold an overview toward potential consequences and retribution. Whenever we do something that is misaligned with our true Nature, we are forced to re-evaluate our behaviors—because we cannot survive two opposing forces within us. We cannot endure the wrath of delusory ambitions gone awry.

The only strength we can lean upon is the inner powers of kind restraint and precious acceptance. In a personal commitment to our lovely Self, we begin to embrace the world that we ache for, a peaceful world, because we cannot be in a world that is unlike us.

To create a peaceful society, we act with quiet self-assurance. We live centered in serenity. We tend to our longing for affection so that it does not go awry.

When centered in the quiet space of our eternal being, nothing can shake us and our personal values remain aligned. When centered in our inner power, the effect of the outer world cannot disturb us. When aligned with our inner ruler, we are able to maintain our true presence in the world.

To live successfully in the world *and* indulge in its expectations, we clear out of our psyche the duality of our intentions. We find a reference point within ourselves from which we can discern between what is good for us and what essentially would devour our goodness.

At some point on the soul path, we all face this.

5

How to Recognize Truth and Genuine Persons of Light vs. Cults, Liars and Charming Manipulators

Seeing Beyond People's Facades

At all stages of the process of spiritual access to your inner being, you have the inner *knowing,* already. You have the ability, already, to feel and choose clearly: to discern whether a particular study, path, book, teacher, guru, guide, psychic reader, minister, church, or group of any kind is giving you the freedom to experience them without any expectation and without demanding of you your total commitment to their cause and only their cause.

The easiest way to discern the true intentions of any other person is the inner connection or feeling you have on your first encounter with that person.

Wisdom increases with experience, and psychic sensitivity enhances with practice. However, at all times, you have the ability to critically analyze the effect of any ideas on your emotions, even when you are just beginning the soul path or not even there yet.

You have the ability, already, to observe your intuitive senses. They are God in you guiding you. No one else can guide you. When you focus on your inner alignment, you can *feel* with whom to participate and from whom to learn.

When beginning the soul path, it is wise to be cautious about what teachings you allow to influence you and what human teachers you choose to acknowledge as wise, because some teachers are not living in the light. It is important to learn—early on—how to discern which studies will help you and which could cause you confusion or a loss of your soul power.

Some avenues that call themselves "new age" are, in fact, hype; they are even misleading and dangerous. Examples of this are groups or persons that demand control. If anyone ever demands that, for you to be "saved" or to be a part of their "following" or to be ensured of safety (in their domain) or to get to "heaven," you must follow their commands of behavior, be assured: They are either consciously attempting to control your emotions and mental judgments or they are themselves confused about the source of their power.

Teachers of light do not demand that others do their bidding. They do not attempt to confuse anyone with promises of "gold in heaven" while expecting others to give over all of their "earthly possessions" to them or the "congregation." Proponents of salvation who are in the light ask only what you personally choose freely for yourself. Be extremely cautious about any person who proposes that you give over your money, home, or family; or that you give up your personal ability to choose or change your mind.

The criteria for discerning whether anyone is giving you sound advice is your first impression about that person and your first reaction about the ideas given. If you sense subterfuge or manipulation, most likely you are correct. However, if you sense in the person a deep commitment to higher truth, that person may be sincere. Even so, look more deeply at the teachings. The ideas can still be unclear and marked by spiritual immaturity.

A person who is making every effort to live a life of goodwill and personal presence—with fairness, humility, and good sense—*is* ready to lead others. You can trust a person who teaches that only you can choose and only you must. How can you tell the difference?

When beginning the soul path, the difference is vague and you are vulnerable. Ideas that are reliable feel supportive to you, encourage your own analysis, and advise you to choose freely from various sources of insight.

Learn from people who give *you* the power to live your own life freely. Learn from people who ask *you* to be your own person. Learn from people who insist that *you* listen only to your own Inner Counselor for direction.

It is gravely important to acknowledge your own unique power and to see that *you* are a person of value in your own right. Acknowledge your own perceptions, listen to your own heart, and accept no other person's command over you.

The power of higher consciousness is a gift everyone is able to access. Becoming enlightened is natural to human evolution. Every person is innately linked to the Divine Consciousness. By following the path of spiritual self-realization, you tap into the Self you already are and uncover your *innate* intuitive knowing. Following the soul path is a process of remembering what you already know.

When studying various books, going to various classes and listening to various teachers, remember: Only *you* are the decider of your life. Only *you* are able to choose most wisely for yourself. Only *you* can live the purpose for which you exist and for which you were born, because only you can truly know it.

Teachers of light guide and inspire. Teachers of light applaud your own revelations. Teachers of light hold *you* up as their equal in the pursuit of higher knowledge. Teachers of light accept you as their equal, because teachers of light know that everyone has the same access to the "truth."

The difference—the only difference—between you and any teacher is the level of understanding, which is acquired over time from *experience*. Experience does add to wisdom, yet every person begins with the same amount of understanding.

All of humanity now have access to the ancient mysteries. What was once known only to a few is now easily known by anyone traveling the inner way.

There is no outer instructor. We are each our own instructor. Teachers of light guide you to be strong and self-reliant. They are guided by Spirit rather than by intellect or ego. Teaching is their true purpose in life. They believe in themselves, and they believe in you.

Teachers of light glimpse your true being. They forgive errors, and they allow others to believe differently than they do. They forgive the complications of being human.

Teachers who live the inner light are resolved to being of service in any way they can. They open their hearts and minds to all paths of study. They are nonrestrictive and nonexclusive. They invite all attitudes and perceptions of thought. They make no demands or commands that any other person must obey. They allow you to contribute and study as you feel guided to do from within yourself.

A teacher of light *may* place some restrictions on you. However, any suggestions made are from the Universal Consciousness and are *recommendations* for your beneficence. It is always your *choice* whether to integrate such principles in your own lifestyle. Teachers of light give tools and insights for you to make your own evaluations. They challenge, guide, and instruct. In some ways, this can be demanding. Yet at all times you are free to choose.

Some guidance given through a teacher of light may have to do with healing your physical body to help you at all times be at-one with your spiritual Identity. You also are instructed on how to heal and let go within your emotional body so that you will not be controlled by desires, arrogance or a sense of failure; and so that you will not deny your ability to analyze, discern, and choose. You also are guided to see things mentally clearly and to discern the nuances of truth from untruth—which is *felt*.

All of this is part of becoming at-one, teaching you how to enhance every aspect of your being and how to integrate in order to function as a single unit. This takes practice.

A teacher of light has knowledge and also access to wisdom . . . and knows the difference. Your responsibility is to choose teachers and counselors who will share with you their own experiences, perceptions, and understanding about universal truths.

When beginning the soul path, we subconsciously choose a set of laws and principles that will be least strenuous to our personal beliefs about the laws of nature and will *most* enhance our life experience. As we mature in sensitivity, we acquire a more sophisticated and subtle understanding of cosmic laws. We become more and more capable of self-disciplining ourselves and acquiring attitudes and belief structures that are attainable when we are willing to let go of the obtuse processes that have held us back. Whatever the principles are, which we may study *prior* to accepting them, we do come to understand them.

Understanding the difference between teachers of light and those who are misguided helps you to discern people who preface their teachings with the right words and right concepts yet their actions indicate the opposite. Teachers of light allow you to follow your own way. Their teachings are suggestions (recommendations) deferred to *your* own free will.

6

Our Resilience Sees Us Through It

How to Survive the Challenges of the World

The first exercise in acquiring the inner connection to our soul consciousness is to accept without limit our ability to ascend into higher awareness. In this attitude, we are blessed by the presence of the angels.

On the path to higher awareness, we learn to appreciate the angels' presence—until their point of view becomes our own. Once we are aware of the angels as a force guiding us, we increase in knowledge about the higher realms of being, and we grow in understanding about our own ability to attain higher wisdom.

For this reason, humanity is now being flooded with insights about the presence and power of the angels.

At first, the angels inspire us. They begin speaking into our heart as we awaken from lifetimes of unconsciousness about our true Self. They divinely increase our sense of motivation to improve our personality and to resolve our concerns about being human and in a body that dies.

So the *first function as an aspirant* is to accept that angels live and present themselves in our consciousness when we are awakening to our soul. It is a great moment in the aspirant life when we realize the potential power of the angels. Not only do they offer us protection, which they can indeed give when we follow the laws of nature; they also encourage us to stay on the path of goodwill and to serendipitously *share* with others.

~ ~ ~

The angels in my own life have been several, although I've not always been aware of them. As I look back, however, I can remember the very particular circumstances when angels were present as a force of encouragement to me. They even caused me to go in the direction of consciousness I now appreciate. Without the angels' encouragement, I would not be the person I am today. I would have given up, because the challenges of life were so overwhelming, misguiding me into believing not in myself but in the unnameable forces that at the time seemed to control me.

This, of course, was not the reality, but that is how I felt. Even during the years when, as a child I was incested by my father, even then I was instilled with a determination to overcome the burden of that time. Despite the immeasurable psychic suffering, somehow I envisioned a potential existence free of the false belief that I was not good or good enough.

Gratefully, I was carefully tutored (on the inner planes) by my Higher Self and angels. I am certain that without their help through *inner promptings,* I would not be alive today. I would have died a long, long time ago, out of despair and out of the belief that I could not hold up under the strain. First, the incest. Then the family sending me away and blaming me. Later in life, enduring a domestic abuser—until I finally found my voice.

You may feel this way yourself at times. If so, I encourage you: Hold on. And I remind you (from my *inner knowing self*): You *are* strong and you *can* be exactly the person you imagine, because that is exactly the person you were born to be.

I have learned that life truly is up to us. No matter what happens, *we* determine how an experience will affect us. We determine whether an experience, such as a death or abuse or a loss of any kind, will be a central issue that controls every moment we exist—or whether we will be free of that burden on our heart.

It isn't what happens to us that determines how we turn out or what our life is like. No matter what happens, we can change the way we think about ourselves and about others. Indeed, this is the only way we can have a life with any measure of joy.

It isn't that we must accept any other person's wrongdoing toward us. We don't so much forgive that person's actions, as we forgive ourselves for being unsuspecting and innocent.

It also is not our responsibility to carry any other person's "weight" . . . unless we have an absolute inner knowing that being that person's instrument of correct reflection is right for us to take upon ourselves, and all that goes with it.

Our responsibility is to heal only our own suffering and our own pain. We do this by letting go of the need to prove, in the eyes of the person who caused us so much grief, that we are worthy.

We are born worthy. Every person is born worthy. Worthiness is innate in being human.

We also each have a purpose in life that surpasses our previous experiences. We were born with a purpose. When we apply ourselves to being attuned to the inner light that is inherent in us, in time we do become aware of that purpose.

I share a bit of my past as an example of how it is possible to attain the *inner resonance,* despite our experiences.

I have tended to be gullible, naïve and over-enthusiastic, always hoping for the best, always wanting to believe in a person's potential and to believe what the person says rather than what the person does or observe that person's energy. This has gotten me into trouble many times.

I have learned to forgive my periodic bouts of unconsciousness, because I know I am doing all I can to be fully aware. Discernment is a lesson we learn in different stages. It is one of life's *adventures.*

Discernment is trusting your instincts. Trust your first impressions—your first automatic, spontaneous, emotional, gut reaction (not what you wish were true). Sometimes it is best to know that a particular person or situation does not warrant our attention. Sometimes it is best to walk away. On the other hand, it may be absolutely right to stay and only *you* know which it is—by your *gut feeling.*

Human beings are all about stretching. We are constantly in a state of growth. We are fascinated with our challenges and opportunities. We want to do better. We want to solve.

Despite our resistance to change, we constantly create change. Plus, change is always upon us. Change is the nature of the Creative Force, thus the nature of our lives.

So, this journey of the soul path (spiritual path) is not some illusion or mystical escape from reality. It is *reality.*

We survive the trauma of the world by linking to our soul strength. As we nurture that part of us, it becomes more substantially our identity in the world and we become solidly inspired to be the Self we always knew we could be.

I wish for you this *gift of light:* that you are open to your inner encouragement from your soul and the angels who counsel you, that you know you *already* are exactly what you have wished you could be: a *gift of light* to all.

Part II

The Steps That Get You There

7

Ten New Universal Laws

Students on the spiritual path generally embrace neither the teachings of a single human nor the teachings of their original religion, but the Creative Consciousness that resides in the center of the human heart. These students study many teachers in order not to be misled as have been millions of aspirants. Rather, these students know that truth varies by the individual and cannot be designated for all except for a few essential attitudes upon which all else may rest.

For those of us who wish to reach past dogma, there are ten basic attitudes of consciousness given from the Divine Mind to make life easier for us to live. These universal truths are a personal strategy for how to live successfully and peacefully. In esoteric studies, says the Divine Mind, these tenets of tranquility are called the *"Tenets of Clear Being."* Listed on the next page.

Tenets of Clear Being

- *Be in the moment that you are.*

- *Be exactly where you are.*

- *Acknowledge your highest level of being.*

- *Appreciate yourself.*

- *Appreciate others.*

- *Exude a clear presence.*

- *Invoke a clear conscience.*

- *Honor the highest range of affection.*

- *Live in the beliefs of goodwill.*

- *Give of yourself when needed.*

When we exercise our personal will to actually practicing the "Tenets of Clear Being," we are embracing the ten most basic components of peace of mind: because we are then free of distress and inner persecution, and we are more devoted to the whole. We *learn* to believe in the All of life.

Students of esoteric teachings, says the Divine Mind, often forget that ritual is a tool for accessing the Cosmic Mind and that ritual is not otherwise a useful power. However, when we do exercise the powers of ritual, potentially we can be a presence of positive influence on others. In fact, says the Divine Mind, the use of any ritual does unconsciously affect us. Whether or not we understand a ritual, its powers do shape our thoughts.

The "Tenets of Clear Being" are a ritual for the full state of being we all seek to engage. The Tenets open in us a vivid comprehension of how to live harmoniously. At the same time, the Tenets set a discipline of universal truths to clarify our evolving sense of self into being a person of wholeness and goodness. For of what use are any personal tenets, if not embraced for the well-being of all?

The consequences of exploring the inner path result from our personal evolution. The inner path cannot bring any kind of outer perfection without our personal commitment to a central attitude of goodness; because all persons struggle between desire and inner knowing, and everyone wishes to be faithful to spiritual law.

However, without personally committing to living by an attitude of goodness, we tend not to be strong enough to uphold right thought and right action. We tend to suppress reason in favor of colorful emotions and to kindle superiority as a god; we favor ideologies more than clearly accept other people as they are.

On the path of spiritual survival, when earnest in our dedication to the whole, we continuously strive to more exactly apply the basic attitudes of goodness (the Tenets), which benefits not only us but others.

How can you know when you have acquired clear understanding? You do not need to ask. You know.

As we evolve on the inner path, what do we know? We know that *all* are God, that all are equal, that not one person is more highly endowed than another. We know that the only source of wisdom is the inner realm, which is accessed through self-acceptance.

Once we have begun to integrate the multitudes of teachings of the various reality experts, we begin to understand what they are saying. Once we have released the desires of the body, we begin to see clearly. Once we have acquired the inner power of self-acceptance, we begin to see all things just as they are.

Everyone is on the soul path already, says the Divine Mind. No one has a map for this journey of the inner path of personal surrender to the Universal Presence within. Others can provide to us only a few insights for some understanding along the way. Synergy of the concepts comes when we completely commit to always seeking a more clear understanding, which is mysterious to the uninitiated but primary to the novice who is studying the universal wisdoms. The answers we seek come through our own process of becoming. Answers come through our own revelations and insights. The answers are *within* us.

Every step we take is carefully tempered by the Guardians of the Light: our own Higher Self and our personal entourage of angelic beings. Every thought, every choice, and every decision we make is matched by a higher law. Every situation we find ourselves within is couched in an adventure of self-discovery. Every relationship we experience is an opportunity for self-analysis and self-love.

When embracing truth, we are more accurately being receptive to the Unnameable. We are being receptive to all that is Unspoken. We are then free in our beliefs and without conditioned reflexes, and we are not beholden to any but the right response in each circumstance. Once we have begun to truly perceive our goodness, we are able to conceptualize and intuit right thoughts and right actions. Until then, we are still learning.

It is wise to keep our heart open to all avenues of higher expression. It is wise to realize that each path is true and may offer a glimpse of the greater reality. It is wise to acknowledge the inner truths that abide in each outer spiritual or religious devotion. It is essential to love all of our experiences as a part of our process toward becoming whole.

When beginning the soul path, we are deluged by self-criticism. Mistrust blinds us and we resist the quiet power because we have grown used to our tantrums. We are ignorant of the Presence of the inner realm and unable to fathom a solution.

When beginning the path of inner surrender, we allow our old ways to die. We do not fan them, nurture them, or think on them. By our commitment to the soul path, we come into serenity and self-empowerment—without the need to resist opposing beliefs that might threaten our serenity or shake our confidence.

Many people are bombarded in childhood with messages of doubt or inferiority, so that they disconnect from their Inner Counselor and become a shadow of themselves. This effect becomes like a lampshade blocking their light, so that their only contribution to the culture is a dim reflection of their actual Self.

The Divine Mind advises:

To instill the power of being a spiritual adept, initially grow in a protected environment of loving support. Do not display your beliefs where others might challenge them.

The inner flame of the burgeoning spiritual passion does, in time, become a voice of clear reason. In the beginning, however, it is wise not to parade your newfound truths where others might trample upon them or shred your raw confidence.

It is wise to reflect within the inner silence until you grow strong in your own clear presence of commitment. Remain silent until you are sure of your dedication to the realm of light. Live in the inner kingdom.

Once your power is unquenchable, you are able to withstand any abuse of your contentment. In the beginning, however, be still. Be in your own cradle. Listen only to those who, in a quiet way, move through the world without the need to correct any other's wrong. Those who speak the most softly are the ones who carry the power to transform society.

You can be, on this day, all you have strived to be. You need only take the step of personal commitment, a commitment not to these ideas or these pages, not to any one person, concept or structure, but a commitment to yourself . . . to who you are in your own fullness.

8

How Being Aligned with Your Higher Consciousness Frees Your Optimism

The purpose of being aligned with our higher consciousness is to improve in our ability to heal not only our own suffering but the suffering of others. When we are perceptually centered in our new consciousness, we are able to repair not only our own scars of the psyche but also the scars of others. This is a spiritual responsibility. Once we become enlightened—bonded with our soul—that is when we become of real use to the world and essentially responsible for helping others. This also more clearly defines who we are.

As we consciously expand, we learn to be creative. We tap our whole Capacity for being uniquely gifted in whatever ways are our particular talents and insights into the human experience. As a self-realized person, we are able to attain a level of imagination greater than we have ever known. We are able to do essentially all of those things we have worked on in our many previous lifetimes. As we attune, the depth, breadth and range of our expertise enhances . . . and our imagination becomes limitless.

The Causes of Increased Intelligence

1. Respecting All

The first cause of increased intelligence, says the Divine Mind, is respecting all levels of consciousness.

We also appreciate the further abilities of our own consciousness and our new inner comprehension. We allow ourselves to be fully endowed by the spirit of God, which is everything of which we are capable in that moment; and we resolve to apply every ounce of our attention to fulfilling our natural and inherent abilities.

2. Selfless Service

The second cause of increased intelligence is the death of the ego. We no longer act from a need to satisfy our intimate yearnings. All of our attention pivots to the essential knowing of our whole Self. We no longer resist being of service and benefit to others. We carry no hatred of any kind, and we are not angry.

This releases an explosion of cosmic awareness through our psyche . . . so that all of our ambitions realign to our soul's will, all of our wishes are now our soul's wishes, and all of our concentration is on the various functions of being a *conscious* human.

3. Embracing Your Higher Calling

The third cause of increased intelligence is when we release our anguish and dismiss the attachments that have bound us to pain.

Once we come into our soul consciousness—without any remnant of regret, hostility, or uncertainty, we are ready to live fully committed to our soul's purpose.

Whatever we have personally desired becomes less important. We are now so completely absorbed in the Vital Consciousness that it actually transmutes our desires into a more pure form.

In this way, we access our full awareness, and we are now able to imagine whatever it will take to creatively stimulate the spark of imagination in others. We are now a light of insight for others, because we no longer value our own opinions more than the opinions of the Divine through us.

Once we have attained this increased level of intelligence, we become more settled emotionally. We no longer feel inadequate. We no longer fear that others will laugh at us or reject us. We explore our Higher Will with a sense of abandon and accept our unique approach to the human experience. We define the human experience in a more practical way.

Conclusion

Anyone can grasp the Higher Thought process. It is a matter of dedication and focus. Once we imbue divine *knowing,* all else falls away—until all that remains is our frankly delineated Self; all that remains is our fully realized decision to be all that we can be.

Once we have acquired this enhanced level of understanding, we refuse to be overwhelmed any longer by our emotions. We no longer care for the notions that used to be important to us. We now see with an inner vision.

Our decision to be our full potential Self is our turning point. Once we acknowledge that we are able to reach the higher reality by way of *thought*—and *action* upon those thoughts—we are there already. By the time we see the possibility, we are there already. By the time we accept the new senses of the Divine, we are already expressing Divine Will.

Once we can imagine a condition as potentially real, in the etheric dimension we have already created that thought form. When we believe we can do something, we create a thought form and that thought form solidifies into physical reality.

As we become more used to this process, we actually *learn* to intentionally create thought forms: through single-minded intention, daring belief in the probable, commitment at all cost, devotion to the idea and manifesting it, and acceptance of Divine Will in the manifestation.

With these elements in place in our psyche, we endow ourselves with all of the necessary ingredients to bringing those ideas into physical reality. We have passed the half-thoughts of our aspirations. We have passed the half-beliefs of our immature self. We have passed the half-commitments of our journeying self. We now stand at attention in the light of our soul, and we are soul-embodied.

We begin to live our soul's consciousness, act upon our soul's will, and perceive from our soul's point of view. We express the inner dimensions creatively—because that is the voice of our soul expressing to the world, and we know that without our soul active in our life we would be void.

How Can You Know Your Soul Purpose?

Can you believe in yourself as a soul-embodied human? Can you relate to the purpose of the *inner* you? Do you know what that purpose is?

Your soul purpose is to:

- Live all of your light.

- Accept that soul is you—the whole you.

- Be so encouraged that nothing can dissuade you any longer.

- Be so wise that you know every choice that is right for you.

Courageously take every step in faith that you actually can be the Self you have glimpsed.

You can be your exponential Self right now. You can attain cosmic consciousness *now*.

Once you accept the divine life as your focus for *how* to behave, you are in a new life. You embrace your full Self wholly and accept *all* that you are. You embrace your past, embrace all that you know you can be, and allow yourself to live your probable Character.

- *As you accept, so you are.*

- *As you believe, so you manifest.*

- *As you act, so you create.*

- *As you think, so you enable the world to think with you.*

41

When our thoughts are the unfiltered thoughts of our soul, our thoughts become the thoughts of society . . . and each vision becomes a vision of the whole. Our vision becomes the vision of the world.

When our actions reflect our soul's consciousness, we are able to see the blessedness in every other human being. When living the purpose of our soul, society supports our dreams, because they are the dreams of all souls.

Consciousness expands, we expand. Consciousness evolves, we evolve. We are evolving. We are evolving into the next level of our humanness.

Exponentially, humanity is ascending into the realm of thought where everything will manifest more easily. Our common expectations will come true more immediately—exactly as we have imagined.

When living the attitude *"I am well and whole,"* all that we imagine comes to us. All that we believe we can manifest, we do manifest.

Society is but us extended. By embracing a divine focus, we put divine concepts into the social strata. By living Divine Will to the best of our ability each day, fully dedicated to that will, we come into a new life; our life is renewed and becomes whatever we wish for it to be. We have only to command our inner resolve and know that what we envision *will* unfold. It is certain.

Today in human history is a time of unparalleled opportunity for personal growth. With devotion to living our Highest Aspect here and now—a spiritual being expressing through a body—so we become.

When you allow the attitudes of your divine Self to affect your attitudes and actions every day, you are *re-identifying* who you are, *reshaping* your behaviors, and *restructuring* your reality . . . in the social strata around you.

When you open your inner door and dedicate to being your whole Self, you become that Self so quickly that you are amazed, awed, grateful. Being in a new life is being in this moment your whole Self fully realized.

We live in an era of increasing self-approval. It is time to be your exponential Self. And you can. It is who you already are.

9

The Eight Petals of Self-Discovery

How We Blossom One Petal At a Time

When we surrender to the process of unfolding to our soul's consciousness, we blossom, much like a rose, one petal at a time. Full of promise, we gradually expand into full and glorious bloom.

Following are the eight *"petals of self-discovery,"* received in the Higher Consciousness.

1. *You understand human frailty and accept it.*

   First, we heal all that has gone before in our life. We remove all past hurts from our unconscious, and we forgive.

2. *Divine wisdom fills your heart.*

   It is then that your destiny becomes clear to you and you become aware of a life purpose you haven't before realized—which involves being a voice of inspiration. This *petal* is an auspicious triumph for your spirit.

3. *You unleash your inner power.*

   You receive "insights" from other than your own mind, revelations you could not otherwise have known. This is an ongoing process. As you are more centered in the power of your light, your insights become more centered in the Divine Will.

4. *You undergo a radical alteration of your beliefs.*

This is a natural evolution of inner healing. You become more attuned to the light of the universal truths. What is real and what is not becomes clear to you.

5. *You awaken to your soul consciousness.*

This can be a period of extremes. You meet your own death of personality. Your individuality clarifies. Your life now has direction. Your emotions clear, which is also an ongoing process. For as long as we are human, we are learning to live by the *inner knowing* rather than by emotion.

6. *You enter the realm of universal teachings .*

... beyond the psychisms of lower thought, beyond even the limited understanding of your new appreciation of soul consciousness. You embody your soul's awareness as a completely integral part of your character. After that, the process of infusing your personality with your soul's consciousness is extraordinary! You develop a perception of the Universal Laws that before were but shadow to you. This is an exciting period and one that continuously unfolds . . . until you reach the seventh *petal* of self-discovery.

7. *You embrace divine consciousness.*

You surpass even your soul's splendid perspective. This is a doorway into an even more clear consciousness, much like a passage into another room. This is the most exacting level of self-discovery. Now you begin to live in full self-honesty and with a full commitment to your destiny.

8. *You fulfill your destiny.*

Many apply themselves to this process for many lifetimes. However, *you* can make real progress on your destiny's unfoldment during this *current* lifetime.

Common ideals of the soul journey are to:

. Remove your personality's blocks that have kept you from believing in your soul power.

. Live from your soul's perspective in all that you do.

. Define your existence by the *inner knowing* that guides you.

. Give back to life all that you understand.

When living these ideals, our soul journey is gentle, and swift.

10

The Five Phases to Becoming Fully Higher Conscious and Being Whole

Our consciousness begins to expand once we accept that our personal responsibility is service to others. Once we embark upon stretching our perception of reality, we are in the phase of consciousness expansion called *"Being whole."* This necessary personal realization is a premise for allowing the inner knowing to guide us.

At first, when acknowledging that we are a whole Self, we forget that we are reprogramming our personality, being influenced by our soul's energy to help us stretch in our universal senses, and being re-evaluated by the humans around us.

When we are ready to be our whole Self, we are able to actualize that part of us that is imbued with the divine awareness we call God. When beginning the soul path, it is essential to be open to various methods of self-realization, because all paths lead to one.

1. Expanding

The first step can be trying. Therefore, our Cosmic Self encourages us to grow gradually in our participation with the various levels of energy exchange, so that we may learn in more subtle ways. In fact, this actually brings us into a greater depth of restructuring than if we experience a multitude of personal interactions.

When we first realize that we are being asked by our Cosmic Self to unfold slowly, it can feel as if we are evolving in slow motion. However, evolving gradually is very helpful when first learning the eternal truths, because we drink these in by a vicarious sensitivity to what is going on around us. It is also more pleasant to learn gradually in order not to be overwhelmed by the extreme polarities of the spectrum of new perceptions and to be more settled emotionally, which is an essential attribute at any level of awareness.

So, when first expanding in cosmic consciousness, our Cosmic Self requests us to explore several paths of personal growth. These can be in any field of human expression. Some examples are the mental arts, including astrology, numerology, and tarot.

You may prefer to free-flow on the inner planes, such as through deep meditation and/or Higher Self channeling to yourself. You may wish to learn skills of human communication, such as toning, chanting, or speaking in tongues. You may wish to contribute as a teacher of light by expressing your current perception of reality to others, such as through writing or workshops. You may wish to enhance the healing of your self-consciousness by embracing various religious beliefs. You may wish to contribute to others what you are experiencing vitally, such as through healing bodies or emotions. You may wish to initiate a practice of daily disciplines to help remold your physical body.

These are a few examples of the many avenues that your Cosmic Self may encourage you to explore, to help you learn the full range of your unique individual talents.

2. Saturation

In the second phase of being whole, we begin to reach a limit or point of saturation that redirects the intensity of our search. We eliminate many of our ruminations about human consciousness as related to our particular abilities.

We no longer explore the vast array of the subtle arts, because we find it overwhelming to spread ourselves in so many directions. In a sense, we feel forced to pull back into our inner reality and to re-evaluate the influences those arts have upon human existence in general as well as upon our own experiences as a human.

For a period of weeks or months, we relapse into our psyche wherein we reconsider the value of the studies we have explored. We sense the effects of each study upon our attitudes as a whole Self and upon our part within the spectrum of universal learning. We re-evaluate the intentions of the various modalities and how we may fit into those by our individual nature.

During this second stage of consciousness expansion, we are more silent than expressive, more within our inner Self than externalized in our search. This gives us the psychic space to be more human and in harmony with the "real" world as a person who has an expanded understanding of the nature of reality.

3. "The Second Awakening"

Once we have re-evaluated the various modalities and narrowed our personal link to one or two, again we expand outward. This phase is called *"The second awakening."*

In this phase, we are truly beginning to be valuable as a sensitive, because we have come through many trials of our own resistance to the meanings of the new concepts and beliefs.

In the previous indulgence, we literally stretched into a new and lighter body because we actually were drinking in the energy of those many possible pathways. Then we retreated to reclaim our clarity. Now fully committed to the process, we are able to discern the elements that amplify our person as well as those elements that do not currently relate to our present talents.

During this third phase, we begin to give freely of our consciousness in order to amplify our feeling of expansion. We are more clear than ever in our conceptual analyzing, more clear in our range of understanding, and more attuned to others who are serving humanity. We more greatly appreciate the human struggle to be spiritual, because we recognize that we are still going through it.

During this process of increasing compassion, we realize that we have much to give and we feel inclined to teach, although not with an intellectual repartee. Rather, our heart is so full from a willingness to share that we cannot hold back being available as a teacher of goodwill. We allow others to come to us with their troubles, and we comfort them in their pain, not with shallow or superficial ideas but with a caring presence. We embrace them with new courage, and we listen.

During this stage, we become a seer, healer, or counselor. We greatly expand in our senses. We see each person in his or her total presence. We do not offer solutions. Rather, we assist others to re-evaluate their own options. We actually see ourselves as less important than ever before, because being of use matters to us now more than what we have to say. We merely accept that somehow we can help others because of what we have learned during our own struggles.

4. *"The Return into the One"*

After a time, which varies from person to person, we leap to the next phase of cosmic consciousness called *"The return into the one."*

Again, we retreat. But this time not because we feel oversaturated. Rather, we feel drawn inward to embody a deeper level of the Universal Consciousness.

At first, we spend a great amount of time in silence. We journey the inner planes, both mentally and out-of-body in our astral body. We slow down in our outer commitments. We sink into the center of our being. In this way, we truly expand into comprehending the reality of the cosmic whole, because on the inner planes we can understand the overall spectrum more easily. We can more easily hear the Inner Counselor as well as the subtle voices of angels and ascended teachers.

Once we enter this phase of attaining cosmic consciousness, we embrace the deeper themes of spirituality. We are no longer concerned with the various paths and modalities. We evaluate our human self from a more whole appreciation of the finer aspects of life that influence who we are.

During this fourth stage, we devote ourselves to a particular avenue of the inner way. In whatever way that is apparent to us, we go into that study of introspective analysis in a very deep and committed way. Our entire existence becomes a part of our evaluation process. All of our time and focus become deeply imbued by our deeper senses. Nothing we do is without this attitude. Everything we do becomes an expression of our spiritual Self.

This process profoundly amplifies our inner synthesis; because, while embracing this level of being, we also feel a tremendous resistance to the ways humans generally behave. We find annoying the severe distinctions between what we see and what we understand life is supposed to be. In a desire to be free of the down side of being human, we wish to avoid the world and we do all that we can to be spiritual because we cannot abide the strangeness of the world. We want only to drink in the cosmic juices of higher realization.

5. Back in the World

Eventually, our spirit is full. Eventually, we accept that to be of the spirit means also to be in the world. When we come back into being a part of the world, our outlook toward human existence is unlike any attitude we previously could understand. We feel more serene. We are more accepting. We embrace life's discontinuities with gentleness. We are not thrown off center. We remain centered. We are a perfect example of rectitude. We give of our presence in a knowing way. We simply are.

During this fifth phase of being whole, we come to accept our humanness. We no longer resist. We no longer hate being human. We no longer wish to leave this world. We have learned that being human is a means of learning greater compassion.

With a new appreciation for the challenges of life, we accept our human level of being for the opportunities it gives us to express our divine abilities and knowledge. We no longer exacerbate. We no longer frustrate. We are equanimous.

We have released the feeling of being separate. We have released letting emotions rule us. We accept the inner path as a stillpoint around which all else in our life anchors. We invoke the power of our spiritual center in all of our actions and decisions. Nothing about our human experience is separate from our spiritual life. We are living our light. In this way, we are one with all of humanity.

Conclusion

In the journey on the path of attaining self-awareness, we evolve in stages. We go within, we carry this outward. We go within, we expand in our influence. We go within, we share our light. We go within, we are our divine Self on Earth. We go within, we live from our inner reality. We go within, we help others sense their inner reality. We go within, we live for the whole.

The process of becoming self-aware is an upward spiral of the involution and evolution of the living force. In the same rhythm as the cosmic universe of which we are all a part, the evolving process is to flow in and out as breath, in and out as a tide. This rhythm is eternal.

We go within, listening to our heart, our inner being. Then we go without, observing: observing others and observing ourselves with others. We synchronize with the life force that pulses through us. We release all that we have learned, all that we have come to know and desire. We journey unencumbered by predilections, predispositions, expectations. We flow inward and outward as our inner being guides us. We explore whatever we feel guided to explore. We do not ask questions, because we have no need for answers. We merely observe and contemplate. We now find life on the spiritual path abundantly challenging. We no longer succumb to our lower appetites. We no longer give in to apprehension. From a higher perspective, we see and feel from a vantage point that is both discerning and daring to discover who we truly are.

Part III
Embracing Your Soul Self

11

The Key to Personal Certainty

We come to realize that we can be all we wish to be, that we can imagine a probable existence *and* become the Self able to create it.

At first, this may seem impossible, like a fantasy. Yet everything we envision, and to which we apply ourselves, does become exactly what we wish.

The key is being so centered in our certainty that nothing can sway us from our objective, so absolutely convinced that nothing can alter our dream, so confident in our inner being that nothing can destroy our ambition.

When we hold our focus with a constancy of thought, attend to our dream with a personal conviction of its validity, and take the steps necessary that will lead us to the results, whatever we dream *will* manifest, says the Divine Mind. This is why it is vital to shape and direct our thoughts clearly, because *all* that we think—in this potent way—does come to pass, both positive and negative.

It is true that events do not always mirror our mental pictures. But events do mirror our *emotional* sense of what we want. Events replicate the degree of our conviction and the clarity of our vision. The more confident we are, the more command we have over the cosmic principles that rule nature. The more certain we are, the more accurate are the results. The more imaginative we are, the more creative is the manifestation . . . and it appears to be extraordinary!

~ ~ ~

Let me tell you how this book came to be published. First, I knew with my whole being that this would be. Any doubts I had I quickly *cancelled*. I refused to submit—any longer—to my unreal lower self. I convinced myself that my goal would be realized by devoting myself to it.

With a daily attunement to my vision, I diligently and dutifully absorbed the vision into myself as if it were the very air I breathe. I infused my conviction so deeply that it became a part of me, filling all of my thoughts at all times. Whether I was taking a walk, attending a function, or visiting with a friend, I was completely focused on the end result. I spent all hours available every day in the process—creating new texts, revising existing texts, proofreading, editing, studying, attuning, meditating. Everything I did was a part of the process—until I was no longer separate from the goal. The vision was merely an extension of my being, as real and tangible as my physical senses.

In this very concentrated focus, my abilities improved and the scope of my previous capabilities magnified. With total attention to the vision, I found myself essentially able to write nonstop on several different projects simultaneously, limited only by my physical body's needs, such as food and sleep. I reached the apex of my potential. I seemed to fly through the long but exhilarating hours as if on the crest of a wave. It was ecstasy! In this awesome level of my greatest-ever capacity to clearly describe my experiences and allow the philosophies flowing through me from the Cosmic Mind, I was incredibly centered, like a rock, unshakable. It was truly fantastic!

The further I progressed with this manuscript, the more certain I became that something concrete would result from my continuous concentration, that my dedication indeed would bear fruit. And it did.

This process of *thought-desire-application* became the model for the other aspects of my life. Once I found the key to unlocking the seeming phantom of my long-held dream, I was able to retain the key. I was able to continually apply myself because of the initial thrust. I had actually worked the principles for so long—seven months consistently[1]—that they became a part of my personality make-up. I broke through my uncertainty, self-doubt, and lack of faith, and released to the potential I had always felt was within me.

My *love of the work* was the second cause of the result. Not only did I truly and earnestly want a particular consequence, but I loved the writing fervently in my very soul—as if it fed me (and it did, and does each time I read this book and the other writings). I so embodied the *inner urging* that it totally filled me with its senses of exquisite satisfaction.

Nothing will ever equal for me the fulfillment of being aligned with the creative powers of life so that they streamed through me unstoppable. I felt as though I could write eternally. And I can—in *this* voice—because *this* voice is within me and flows from my pure heart.

So, the two causes toward manifesting what is dearest to us, says the Divine Mind, are our belief in the probable outcome and our love of what we do. It is not enough to want something. We must *become* it in all aspects of our being. We must embrace it until it is all, until everything we do expresses the vision and is an extension of it.

Every day we create our own reality. Before we awaken our spiritual inner Self, we create and manifest unconsciously, resulting in obscure and often unpleasant circumstances. As we learn to discipline our attitudes and beliefs (the effects of our thoughts and emotions), we learn to control the affirmations of our desires. As we become more clear in our focus, more certain in our objectives and more aligned in our consciousness, the results that manifest in the outer world reflect more accurately what we have envisioned.

Some people do this without realizing it. They already learned this skill in some area of their lives. Some people take longer, but everyone is able, says the Divine Mind. We are able to clearly draw to us what we command from our *inner knowing self* in all areas of life: finances, career, even relationships.

---

1   1994.

Being *commanding* is an acquired skill, says the Divine Mind. As we mature into how to be insightful and self-imposing, we learn the rudiments of the ability to *command*. As we hone the outer techniques of our particular vision (for me, learning grammar and practicing writing), we eventually evolve past the preliminary stages until we become expert.

Some people are exceptionally gifted in their ability to grasp the elusive power of self-will and to achieve seeming miracles without apparent effort. Most people, however, strive toward this all of their lives, applying themselves diligently every day. But, be sure, self-realization and self-assurance go hand-in-hand, says the Divine Mind.

So, to create the reality of your fondest dream and your most sacred Self, *how* you put your attention to it determines the result, because *we are what we think.*

When your thoughts and images are muddled, what manifests is less like you envisioned. The more precise and clear your focus, the more accurate the effect in the physical world.

We clearly and accurately manifest our soul's desires by our regular focus and practice of them. The degree of our attention determines the degree of the result.

Everyone innately has a full imagination, a clear heart, and a commitment to rival even the best of geniuses. Everyone has access to the creative power of the Cosmic Mind . . . and we all can *grow* our intelligence and our imagination, says the Divine Mind. All we have to do is use it. Stretch it. Learn the key, then do it. Doing seems the greater task, yet I assure you it is easy when in your heart you know you must.

We become attuned to the inner path by realizing what we value. We are affected by what we believe because our self-image is shaped by our perceptions of who we are. This is based upon our own impressions but also upon what others tell us. In truth, we are each much more than we have imagined.

To stretch into the higher perception of yourself, instill a *pattern* of thought and behavior that reflects self-discipline; and trust your inner promptings to be more than you have been. The process of reconstructing your self-image increases your confidence in your ability to become what you have dreamed you can be.

The results of increasing self-discipline appear to be almost mystical. It is more accurate to say, however, that repeated practice toward your new Identity results in the Self you want to be.

When we accept that we are not unique, we actually diminish our spark of originality. When we accept that we do not make a difference, we become indifferent and, in this way, succumb to the belief that nothing matters. When we believe that we cannot become what we imagine in our dreams and desires, we can become lost in depression; in fact, this is suffering from self-denial, because our yearnings are the voice of our soul guiding us toward our destiny. When we accept that we are under restraint, we are being overwhelmed by a prevailing group consciousness, which is more the cause of our failure than our desire untended.

Our own personally envisioned self-image does shape our experiences in life. For this reason, our *inner knowing self* encourages us to rely on the inner voice of goodwill rather than on outer voices that lack enthusiasm for our imaginings.

When you believe that, no matter how things appear, you are capable of fulfilling your most sacred dreams, you are. When you *believe* . . . it is inevitable that you will find a way to culminate every potentiality you envision—because what we imagine **is** possible. What we devote ourselves to becomes our reality; because when aligned with the purpose of our soul, our vision directs our ambition.

Your own perfect reasoning—in your higher consciousness— reveals the necessary steps toward their achievement. Your own reasoning process eliminates less likely alternatives and inevitably directs your whole being, in attitude and action, toward completing the self-fulfilling prophecy of becoming everything you have felt you can be.

When we feel insecure, confusion and an inability to imagine result and we become bogged down by our own intrepid formulas for failure. When we accept the prevailing attitudes of society that possibility is limited, we become unable to understand the necessary wisdom for living all of our potential.

However, when we understand that the attitudes around us are not the true impression of *our* inner Self, we strive more definitively toward becoming what we have imagined *is* possible.

Once we infuse our personality with the unwavering confidence of the *inner knowing,* we begin to raise our potential actions toward a very clear destiny.

If we achieve success at our own expense, of what real value is it? Can we acquire all that the world insists is important and be delivered immaculately from our dreams and still remain sane? We cannot. We can, however, acquire a perfected self-image by understanding that, although living in the world is a challenge, we truly are able to achieve our objectives.

When you surprise yourself repeatedly with outstanding accomplishments in your most secret and private desires, you learn to trust that your inner voice, which prompts you, is in fact your own good Nature inspiring you in the very endeavors that are your God-given talents for being fulfilled and for fulfilling your life purpose.

When attuned to your *inner knowing self,* you do not listen to any other person who denies your *knowing* of reality. You rise in your own perfect insight. This gives you focus and encouragement as well as direction for the necessary processes to achieve the state of mind that will lead you to manifesting your desires. When you inevitably accept and act upon your desired goals, they will, in fact, happen at some point, says the Divine Mind.

You cannot restrain a perfect outcome when you devote yourself continuously to an objective. When you feel directed by your *inner knowing self,* it is because you have the ability to fulfill that perceived image. When you agree with your *inner knowing self's* perceptions of who you can be, and apply all of your attention to finding a way of bringing that Self into your "real life," undoubtedly you will manifest that Self at some point in this life—because we are what we believe ourselves to be, says the Divine Mind.

What attitudes, beliefs, and values might restrain you from perceiving your purpose?

If we cannot acknowledge that our soul and angels are real, we cannot hear the inner voice. If we dismiss all avenues of spiritual exploration, we can be blinded by an ignorance of the nature of life. If we accept that we lack vision, we cannot conceptualize otherwise. If we believe we are surrounded by inexplicable forces that control our destiny, we cannot understand how to tap the life forces or access control as a powerful, self-directed being. If we are overwhelmed by society's wants of us, we are out of balance and we lack inner direction. If we succumb to believing that the prevailing social attitudes are the "norm," we are denying the true nature of life—because *all* that exists manifests out of the etheric realm of Mind.

However, when we realize that the journey of life is a process of becoming aware of our true Nature—our inner Self—we open a door *within* us that inevitably will reveal the way to discover our purpose and how to fulfill it.

What we *think* ultimately does become our reality—in our experience. This is a basic law of nature. What we *think* is truth for us. Regardless of how little it may be truth for others, it is our own perceptions that shape our experiences in life. Whether we flow or suffer is due to our basic attitudes toward the conditions around us. If we accept that our efforts are futile, we are lacking the vision necessary to change our circumstances. However, when we trust our Inner Counselor—which prompts us with certain attitudes, notions, imaginings, and ideas—and we act upon those revelations, we find a way to bring forth that very result.

The solution to what pains you is the inner values you carry, because those values direct your vision of what is real and acceptable in the eyes of all. When you ultimately believe in all inner wisdom that comes to you from your soul consciousness—as well as from angels and Ascended Teachers—you are willing to consider possibilities. This is a good beginning toward awakening the inner vibrancy of the creative mind.

Although we apparently came into this world by accident, our getting born was no accident. To whom we were born was no accident. Where we were born was no accident. Every element of our existence, we *predetermined*.

Although the environment into which we were born may have been, in our perception, negative or positive, prior to being born we envisioned the potential growth of our soul and what experiences would shape us into our whole and ideal Self. Our soul instructed us toward the particular environment within which we could become inspired to our true destiny as a soul-embodied human.

How we view our experiences is the *first ingredient* of defining our Character toward our ultimate achievements in life. How we respond to our circumstances is the *second ingredient* that directs the unfolding of our Character. How we choose to be in the continuously expanding environment of life determines whether we will achieve our soul's purpose or not.

If we deny our inner cries for personal exploration to satisfy the inexplicable yearning of our being, we are not acting upon our soul's purpose: which is our essential reason for being alive.

However, when we do accept, allow, and perhaps even invite higher learning into our sensitive self-image of what is possible, we are embracing the greater possibility that inevitably will become all we have imagined is possible for us.

Ultimately, the greater truth is not what others tell you, expect of you, or believe of you. The greater truth is who you already know you are.

12

How to Know Your Destiny

As you transform the inner,
so the outer will transform.

Even if you do not understand your destiny or recognize the path to follow in a career, relationship or lifestyle, the Inner Counselor does have the clarity to give you the necessary instructions. From the Inner Counselor, you can receive insight into your flaws and weaknesses, as well as your strengths, and receive paradigms to help you creatively unfold your natural intellect. These paradigms then instill you with a vision that is more vast than anything you have previously encountered.

The Inner Counselor informs us of our entire scope of reality, shows us our past-life experiences that directly link with our present life, shows us our future for comprehending the obligations of our inner Self, and gives us elements to develop a clear vision of our character for knowing what is appropriate and what is not for healthful living mentally, physically, and emotionally. When we live with a wrong vision—one that denies our soul power—we are caught between other people's perceptions of truth and the demands of society and our own inner promptings toward a particular pathway.

When we first engage the Inner Counselor, we may be upset because our belief structures are shaken or even destroyed. This process can be gradual or it can feel catastrophic, with a sudden shift in awareness.

Regardless of how your personal soul process develops, the Divine Mind recommends:

- Do not discount the inner advice too quickly.

- Take the advice into serious consideration.

- Give it time to digest in the inner workings of your personality, to realize value in the advice.

- Take time to re-imagine who you are.

Once you do this, it is time to seriously re-analyze your life. What have you been doing? Are you satisfied? If not, it is essential to your whole fulfillment to discard whatever attributes have retarded your sense of being valuable.

My friends, we are in life to learn, grow, and share. When aligned with our *inner knowing self,* we have a sense of self-appreciation without an abundance of "Look at me, how wonderful I am." (Well, maybe in the beginning.)

When aligned with your life purpose and diligently applying yourself to it, you have an aura of self-mastery and a feeling of self-identity. You feel at last connected to your destiny. You may not completely understand all the ramifications, nor how this realization will alter your life; but you feel a resonance with your behaviors, actions, and choices, and you know you are finally on track.

That is how we elect our path in life and how we alter our relationships, activities, career, and creative expression. All of these are part of the life script (how we tell ourselves we live our life). Any aspect that debilitates our sense of appeal to higher thought either needs to be corrected or dismissed, because it is not in alignment with our higher purpose.

Also, just because something is a higher purpose doesn't mean it cannot at the same time be useful, practical, and realistically applied within society. The greater percentage of people who are consciously "walking the path" contribute through organizations and lifestyles that are considerably third-dimensional and mainstream in appearance and structure.

Few advanced souls isolate themselves from society. A teacher is of greater value when walking among humanity and acting within that realm with a full conscience and serendipity of spirit. A teacher is of greatest value who is incredibly dynamic and who maintains integrity in the midst of every outer condition, at-one in both realities simultaneously.

Whatever your destiny, it is probably not to separate yourself from the usual or mundane life. Rather, it is to walk the inner path in the midst of outer experiences. An active lifestyle is not necessarily unspiritual. Your heart leads you in the way you can be of greatest use, aligns you with the sincere vision of your Higher Self, and fulfills your needs and desires at the deepest level of your being.

Being spiritual—soulful—is a point of view, a synergistic approach toward events and circumstances. Being soulful is an attitude that determines your choices and behaviors. Keep an open mind about your interests and activities. Whatever you feel strongly compelled to do from your *inner knowing self* is at least an aspect of your life path, the thread if not the tapestry of your life expression.

~ ~ ~

From the time I was twelve-years-old, I wanted to be a writer. Ever since my fifth-grade English teacher, Mrs. Snodgrass, told me I could write, I felt a yearning to write, even that I must write.

This desire became the directing passion of my entire life. Yet it took many years of self-growth—clearing personality, integrating emotionally, healing pains and wounds of the past (learning forgiveness)—to clearly connect with the expression of my destiny. Throughout my life, I have written, honed the skill, fine-tuned my personality, and worked on healing the scars of my psyche, my heart wounds.

All the pieces eventually came together. I finally reached a point of interlinking. And I didn't even know it was coming. It just happened. About the same time as when I reached the level of skill as a writer when I would finally be of use to others as well as myself, I also reached a point in my personal growth of integrating the various elements of who I am: clearing out the elements that had muddled my self-picture.

All of these aspects reached a point of self-empowerment simultaneously in 1994, May through December. This process has continued. Fortunately, I have been energized by a strong sense of result after my many years of effort . . . and it has been well worth every ounce of commitment and every micro-second of struggle.

When we commit ourselves to a goal and reach it, we have a very strong feeling of accomplishment. Further work to be done on our personality, character, and talents becomes exciting and stimulating; because *then* we know how, we know what we need to do, we have grasped the tools and techniques and it is merely a matter of going through the process. The only thing left is self-will and application, which become easier because these are also learned on the path.

As we become more self-assured and clear as to our personal destiny—clear in our ability to follow-through and act upon what we know intuitively—people come into our life to help us fulfill our destiny. The picture is always getting more clear. We are continuously gathering more pieces of the puzzle and more adroitly fitting the pieces together. Our destiny picture becomes more clear year by year and month by month. Sometimes the process is so heightened that daily, even hourly, we feel the exhilaration of our purpose. The effect is quite stunning!

So, whatever your particular interests and hobbies, whatever your inner Self is prompting you to do, it is very valuable and necessary to your unfoldment and your destiny.

Your inner yearnings are the voice of your soul guiding you. Your conviction that what you seek will come to you is the power that will manifest the result. Conviction puts forth desire, which transforms behavior patterns (likes and dislikes) and will draw to you circumstances, situations, and persons. Certainty brings results!

The first order of truth is to be yourself. How? Just let go. Allow that you are where you need to be *now,* yet that as a creative being you can transcend if you desire. To transcend your present circumstances, allow your creative potential to lead you. To manifest, be true to yourself, to the extent that you understand who you are. Fear not that this is all there is, that nothing else can be done, that nothing else will be right for you. It is not so.

When comfortable with our desires, we feel good: *"I want to do that. That really matters to me. I care about that."* Such insight comes from the core of your being, your essential Self. Such ideas can greatly motivate you. Ideas appear to be opposites, but they are merely different fragments of a same thought. Look for the parallels and harmonies in your thoughts. See how the ideas correspond.

~ ~ ~

A few years back, I became aware of a fear that I was unable to care for myself financially. I felt I didn't know how to achieve success, and I felt betrayed by my upbringing because I didn't learn self-esteem. As an adult, I still felt like a child emotionally. I began to consistently apply the principles that my Inner Counselor had been teaching me, and I finally learned to relax my self-judgments and to trust myself.

During the years of my maturing emotionally, I was a student of the Universal Mind. This helped me to see a broader point of view about life. It gave me an expanded insight and understanding of human nature. I attuned to and bonded with my *inner knowing self* through consistent meditation and through studying truths that had been received by various visionaries, including Jonathan Parker, Richard Bach, and Alice Bailey. These author-teachers, among others, became my mentors for learning to accept my whole Self. Eventually, I came to believe I am a good person because I seek to live positively. I accepted that I have inner strength, and I learned to believe in my soul power.

I still exercise poor judgment at times and allow my unevolved aspects to control my emotions, moods, and attitudes. When I do, the effects are absorbing. I have spent years swinging back and forth. Nevertheless, I have come to understand that this is human and I accept it as a part of my evolving human nature. To counter this, I diligently work at maintaining a Whole Self perspective and at dissolving my limiting behaviors and fears. Ram Dass once wrote that we merely learn to rise above our fears. My formula is: Always come back to center: through the breath and a moment in stillness.

It is easier now to forgive myself as well as to forgive others, because I know that my natural character—my true Self— acknowledges and acts upon the inner knowing that guides me. While I still apply myself daily, I now can more fully accept the process. I am more attuned to the inner planes and more willing to stretch into new areas of potential abilities.

My openness to becoming more has been my true healer. Expanding my perceptions and opening my mind and feelings to self-appreciation has made it easier to forgive my occasional unconscious actions and to appreciate my effort to make right choices, which takes consistent practice. When I am living in the perspective of my whole being—my soulful Self—it is easy to be happy and fulfilled.

Embracing and nurturing my soulful Self has given me an understanding of how all of society can overcome its weaknesses— because I am one in society. My struggle is humanity's struggle. My old fears still lurk beneath my new persona. Resistance to self-assurance still pulls at me. Yet now I know how to move past these when they arise. I know how to lift my awareness to my soulful Self who *is* in peace. I found this by pursuing my inner calling.

Each of us is given specific tasks in life. We each came into life with unique talents. When we dutifully apply ourselves to these talents, we become confident.

Confidence is a byproduct of *living* your destiny. Your destiny is what you feel *prodded* within to do.

When you are "imagining" your potential, you are actually glimpsing your true yearning and feeling the true desire of your tasks in life. You release yourself to your dreams, you stop resisting, and you have the strength to be all you must be. You have courage, and you believe in your vision.

We *learn* not to be afraid. It took me half a century to accept my higher Nature and begin to be it. An open heart is the doorway to inner peace.

When you trust your intuition, you open the door to your soul. The hope you feel is your soul asking to be heard, yearning to be acknowledged.

When you believe in your soul power, you have that power to give . . . and the supply is endless. When you live your soul power, you are fulfilled, because the power of soul is an absorbing force. Soul pulls you totally into its vision, totally into its appreciation of you—until you become fully endowed with the abilities of your powerful *inner knowing self.*

To let go of the restraints that have controlled you, let go to the *vision* within you. You have a vision. You *know* why you are here. That awareness is inborn and instinctive.

If you deny what you sense, you can become despondent. Yet when you are open to exploring your potential, you expand like a flower being filled with the radiant warmth of the sun.

When you relinquish to your soul, you begin to live and be what you were born to be. You begin to move past the fears that have haunted you. You no longer allow others to deny you. You no longer accept that you are incapable of living your dreams.

You have a choice.

In my own life, I have studied, struggled, and cried. Yet now I know *how* to be at peace. Although faux pas still occasionally peek out in my day-to-day experiences, I am more accepting of myself because I *know* I am giving all that I can to the process. I am applying myself completely to the tasks of my inner being.

Compliance with the wishes of your soul leads you to understanding. Compliance with what you want makes what you want reality. When you attend to the desires of your inner Self, what you seek becomes your world.

We create the life we want—by our attention to it. Every day is an opportunity to live as your inner Self and to magnetize to you all the properties that will make it real. To be the Self you envision as ideal, nurture your dreams, act upon them daily, and continuously pursue them—until they manifest. Give all of your attention to your dreams and they *will* come into the world in which you live.

We become what we focus upon. Focus upon being the person you feel you are within and that is the Self you will become. That is the life you will live. It takes time. But it is so.

13

How to Know When to Help Others

You need not change the world.
You need only change yourself.

Appropriate service as a student of the Cosmic Mind is to heed the Inner Counselor's advice, act upon the voice of this *inner knowing self,* and live at-one with that voice—the sacred Self that guides you in choices, decisions, and actions.

Listening to the inner voice awakens that part of you that is eternal and has the ability to perceive all of life from the more clear perspective of your true Self.

What does receiving the wise advice of your inner Self have to do with your present physical life? And how will it affect the way you live?

- You connect to the dreams of your soul.

- You awaken to the yearning that has gnawed at you to heed it.

- You unfold into a being of unequaled splendor, like an ugly duckling becoming a swan, or a caterpillar breaking free from its cocoon as a beautiful butterfly.

- You go forward with a heart that is fully open and a mind eager to stretch into a new way of thinking.

- You venture into a vast inner realm where your capacity is endless.

- You are filled with immeasurable sweetness, and life takes on a clarity and aliveness unlike you have known before.

- You become able to visualize your participation in reshaping the world.

- You grasp contentment and your abundant potential.

- You respect the Vital Consciousness that permeates all of humanity.

- You surrender to your bliss!

- You see the surreal paths of apparently logical realms to which you previously applied yourself in order to satisfy social demands.

- You leap beyond old diatribes. Perceptions of a greater truth pull you out of imagining into the perfect inner poise wherein you tap your reservoir of inner wisdom.

- You feel who you truly can be!

"The Separation from the Outer Mother"

Once we unleash the social restraints of our upbringing, we fathom what we really want, as well as what we are capable of doing.

In the sweet ecstasy of insight, at first we are appalled at the attitudes of outer consciousness and we resist everything that has been our life up until then. This outlook esoterically is called the *"Separation from the outer mother."* We are emboldened to reach a new stratagem, to strive toward an indescribable something. We don't know exactly what it is, yet we feel it continuously pulling at our heart.

You feel a prodding, as if a hand is pushing you out of your safe retreat to explore your lesser understood inner climate.

How can you learn to appreciate society while at the same time nurture your being that is eager to do so much more?

Learn to see society's avenues as a possible way to alleviate the centuries of misunderstanding about why humanity exists. Begin to accept outer reality as a mode for ways to contribute. Even though the outer world is increasingly less tenable to your whole sense of being, it is the realm we are in.

After becoming dissatisfied with life, we begin to understand our soul power and to rethink how to utilize our experiences positively. We rethink our talents as avenues for usefulness in the world. As we become adept at unveiling our inner light, and we more clearly and essentially tap the greater wisdom, our insight becomes more sound and we gain a perspective that previously was unknown to us.

We begin to perceive our true Character with a singular vision. We see our Self that is eternal. We see our splendor, our *godness*. This sets us forever upon the path of service. The fiery transformation of our inner Self erases all that has held us back.

At last, we see the path that is ours to follow. It is whatever suits our personality and our talents. On the soul path, we realize our destiny.

Our soul purpose is the driving force of our whole existence, every step we take. When we take charge of who we are, we become truly free.

Then we go back into the world. We walk through the world alert. We move through the world with clear insight. We are a fortress of inner strength. We maintain a center of tranquility. We evaluate challenges without being drawn into self-doubt. We accept generosity and goodness as our reality.

With a strengthened hope and conviction, we re-enter the social stream, ready to be a beacon for our soul. We stabilize in the community, locally and globally. We reach the apex of our personal power as a light for others to see by, and they are stirred to find and follow theirs.

Our service to humanity is to live our very sure Self in all that we do; to reintegrate in society, because that is where we are needed to actively assist all human brothers and sisters.

When we are clear in our counsel, courageous in our being and in our complete power, we grasp the full potency of our *inner fire*. We are so empowered with living our truth that nothing can distract us, and we overflow with confidence.

Now begins the most useful time of our life and also the most rewarding. We have passed *the turning point*. Now we are drawn into various modes of guiding others in their travels along the soul path.

Eight Criteria for How to Help Others

Following are *eight essential criteria* for how to help others, when to give and when to be silent:

1. *Keep your heart open at all times.*

   Be present whenever circumstances attract you to be involved in some clear way.

2. *Smile, even when suffering.*

   With a clear presence of being at peace, let nothing disturb you. Abide by the "Tenets of Clear Being."

3. *Live sweetness, honesty, and generosity.*

   Be available as a presence of inner beauty and outer representation of that beauty.

4. *Lift their comprehension about their own suffering.*

   Show how things are not as overwhelming as they seem.

5. *Observe.*

   Apply your insights to helping people remedy their own problems.

6. *Incite courage in others.*

   Stir their yearning to explore the inner Self.

7. *Access, through centered clarity, the universal consciousness:*

   This is the source of all essential ingredients needed for any circumstance.

8. *Raise your vibration.*

   Living at all times in the simplicity of spirit, be not overly demanding, nor overly intrusive.

There is no single way to serve humanity. Immerse yourself in being an instrument for the good of all. Respond to the golden thread tugging at your heart. Be a voice for your soul.

What constitutes appropriate service when a student of the Cosmic Mind? What beliefs and attitudes will help you to choose wisely among several opportunities?

To consciously participate in healing humanity, release your whole being to the concept of being a servant to humanity. Kindle your inner Spark to create in you a flame of unrestrained soul passion—until you feel truly honored to be alive!

14

Exercise to Hearing the Inner Voice

Once we ascribe to the "Tenets of Clear Being," consciousness becomes our primary facet of being human—because consciousness is what we are.

The human mind is an aspect of our greater consciousness, and the body is an aspect of our whole consciousness. Essentially, all the forces of nature are consciousness. Animals even are consciousness, as are all plants.

The universal forces abound in many forms. Humanity is one form. Animals, although expressing their consciousness in a different way, are also uniquely aspects of the Divine. They, too, are filled with the inner connection. They understand their own power. They are, as much as we, embraced by the consciousness of the Life Force.

All things that exist are the presence of Thought in its more fully sensed form, which is consciousness. This single element best describes what we humans are and how we are all of *one breath*.

The breath of our being is the Divine Consciousness imbued in us. The breath is the vitality of our presence . . . in a focus of being physical.

Alienation between humans and other species reflects a lack of sensitivity and appreciation of all life forms. Awareness of our inherent relationship with all life forms is necessary for the survival of the human species. Ultimately, in fact, says the Divine Mind, this will determine whether our species will become extinct. Therefore, let us evaluate humanity's role in the cosmic plan.

Human beings are one of several species of a similar organic structure and a similar kind of presence. We are the primary species on Earth because of our ability to *imagine*. If we could not foresee the potential outcome of our actions, or if we could not become the persons we envision in our hearts, we would be little different than the other species on this planet.

However, we have been blessed with a thought process that enables us to think *creatively*. The creative powers are abundant in all of life. On Earth, it is the human species that is able to conceptualize and shape ideas into various patterns and forms, thereby developing new ways to experience ourselves and the world. The human species is consciously aware of its unique ability to transcend its domain, reshape it, and alter it.

Why then have we become apathetic about the inner causative force, as if it is foolish to think we can alter our personal destiny by willing it?

Most humans are abundantly afraid of their soul power. They lack an understanding of it. However, once we realize that every person is a manifestation of the Cosmic Mind, and that everyone can learn to access The Mind, we begin to awaken to the fragmented stirrings of our inner being and we begin to heal the various parts of ourselves. Eventually, we bring these various parts together, united by a central concept:

> "I am an expression of the will of God. That will directs my thoughts and guides me in the purposes of my soul. To that will I hold." — Ascended Master Djwhal Khul (Alice Bailey, *Discipleship in the New Age,* volume one, page 376)

This *attitude* becomes our mainstay of sanity. It shapes our beliefs about who we are and determines the choices we make. It opens our heart and mind to avenues and opportunities we could not see before.

Once we embrace the idea that we are God in form, we begin to access the Universal Consciousness that guides us all and is as much a part of us as our *breath*.

Humanity's inherent nature is to live in kinship with all life forms. When we don't, a fear of the inner power is inhibiting us. Many people become so afraid of their capabilities that they hide from their own passion.

My friends, we are a perfect race just as we are. Although we do, at times, view ourselves with disdain or paranoia, it is valuable to realize that we also have the abilities to imagine, conceptualize, release fears, build dreams, and create a new world for ourselves that is lovely.

It is imperative to realize that our soul power is unalterably linked with the consciousness of the universe we name God. This Presence is a force of goodness that permeates every one of us. Not one of us is void of the Presence . . . and we all have access to its love. We all have access to its wisdom. Each of us can embrace the Divine Presence within our being. It is the hallmark of our full Identity.

When we do not embrace the Divine Consciousness—the very *breath* that we breathe—it isn't because we cannot. It isn't that there is no possibility of ever doing so. Rather, we are choosing in that moment to refrain from believing in our *wholeness*. We are so caught up in our fears and judgments that we become unable to imagine the fullness of life that comes from letting the Divine flow within.

In truth, the Presence is always flowing through us. The Presence is always in us. The Presence is only seemingly absent when we, consciously or unconsciously, block our awareness of it.

We can reclaim this awareness . . . and we can awaken to miracles in our lives. We can be attuned to the softness and the warmth of the *cosmic fire,* which purges us of our inconsistencies.

We learn to do this. The Eternal Thought pervades our entire being. We are more than a body, more than a mind, more even than our intuition. When embraced by the *divine fire,* we *are* the core of its focus, we are the Presence manifest.

How can you attain this clarity of being? How can you learn to hear the inner voice? How can you learn to be aware of the sensations that are constantly passing through you?

Become still.

- Still your body... Still your voice... Still your thoughts... Slow your breath... Slow your rhythm.

- In your mind's eye, hold a picture of the energy of the *divine fire*... See this *cosmic fire* purifying you, healing you, releasing you from pain and judgment.

- Feel the *cosmic fire* moving through you like a gentle whirlwind... cleansing all of your hidden secrets... and bringing you into the light of your own true Self.

How do you do this? *Let go.*

- Let go of the control to which you have fiercely dedicated yourself... Let go of the paralysis of your blessedness... Let go of holding your frozen breath.

- Release the barriers around your heart... Unleash the imaginings shackled by illusions of greed or power... Premise your outlook with an inner awareness of Divine guidance... Release the need to control.

- Allow the Divine Mind to fill you, to flow into your heart and mind ... until you feel its gentleness calming you as a mother soothes the fears of a sleeping child.

The presence of the Divine is as natural as our breath. When we do not release to its solace, we lose the ability to know when the Divine Presence is in us. We lose the sensitivity to recognize the effect of the Divine in our life. We lose the ability to be aware of anything other than the surfaces of life.

We humans are blessed with an ability to consciously interact with the Divine. If we disregard that impact in our lives, we are cutting ourselves off from the very Source of all knowing.

How can you be empowered by this Consciousness?

- Organize your life to make time for connecting with the Consciousness.

- Live each day with an open mind and an open heart.

- Surround yourself with lovely ideas and lovely things.

- Embrace other people and species as your brethren in the cosmic plan.

- Hope. Believe. Trust.

Until we invite the Divine into our heart, we are not living; we are merely subsisting. Once we acknowledge that our own essential being is the Divine Consciousness *in form,* we are open to receiving its counsel. Once we imbue ourselves with the senses and awareness of the Divine Force, we are born into the cosmic oneness . . . and the *fire* of the Eternal begins to blaze within us. This is the beginning of our true life.

15

Sources of the Divine Inner Voice

What is the inner voice? Is that still quiet voice that speaks softly in your mind, your conscience or another being thinking to you? These are concerns of both beginners and advanced students on the soul path.

The inner voice most often is not an external consciousness but is our own Self reflecting to us in a most succinct way—which is the avenue of mystics of all time. When we can hear the inner voice, we are believing in our own divine Nature because, when we can hear the inner voice, we are aligning with our sincere Self, which is the *earliest symptom* that we are restructuring our energy pattern.

Listening to the inner voice is necessary for oneness with our higher Nature because, when we can hear the inner voice, we are able to understand who we are and how to attune to the inborn quiet power. When we are able to hear the inner voice, we are releasing confusion, arriving at personal clarity in our emotions, and becoming more truthful about our faults.

Hearing the inner voice has a powerful effect upon all aspects of our being. To become whole, it is essential, says the Divine Mind, to accept the inner voice as an integral part of the process of our soul development. In fact, hearing the inner voice indicates where we are in the several stages through which we evolve spiritually.

We are also able to hear thoughts projected from other beings, evolutionary *consciousnesses* who exist in different dimensions. There are different kinds of inner voices from whom we receive counsel.

Your Higher Self

First Stage of the Inner Voice Perception

In the first stage of listening within, the inner voice is our own Higher Self. This stage of hearing the inner voice is the most familiar. It is our own Identity speaking to us at a higher level of insight, our own mind revealing to us (generally during a state of drowsiness) insight and counsel that is always instinctively present. This very important stage prepares us to accept the necessary instructions that later will be given to us by Ascended Masters and angels who personally assist us.

This first stage is quite powerful, although continued development eventually will lift us into our higher Nature. However, since the inner voice is very subtle, it is not always perceived. So, the inner voice of the first stage is described here to help you recognize its presence in your mind.

How can you know if you are hearing a thought from your Higher Self? How is that different from your usual self-reflecting and thinking process? Can you, in fact, achieve this connection through practiced *inner hearing?* These are required lessons when beginning spiritual development on the soul path.

The voice of the Higher Self—the most common inner voice—very often is the most pronounced voice we receive. This voice is not the subconscious. The subconscious mind cannot conceptualize its own process. It merely dialects back what it receives from the conscious mind and conscious experience. The subconscious mind does not originate thought. Rather, it is like a computer recording information. When we are in touch with our subconscious, we receive repetitions of already identified information, not new aspects of thought. When we are hearing the inner voice, it is the voice of the supreme aspect of our being . . . and this *voice* is the most perfect reflection of us as an aspect of the Divine.

We exist in several layers of being simultaneously. These are reflected through different aspects of thought or mind. In the beginning, the supreme consciousness is the highest aspect we can hear, aside from direct contact with the Divine, which also speaks in this manner.

Why do we receive counsel in this way? Because often it is the only place we truly listen to our inner secrets and the only time we genuinely accept what we hear.

The inner voice of the supreme consciousness is the most natural experience of the personality. It is the part of us that imagines, identifies new directions, and instinctively realizes opportunities. When we are able to discern the inner voice, we are able to receive our own clear counsel—which is the natural form of the universal wisdom.

The inner voice is the most accurate way by which we humans receive spiritual and life guidance, because it is easier to accept what we are told from within our own mind than from outside ourselves. At the same time, if we cannot hear the inner voice, it is because we are not at that time attuned to our life purpose; we are at that time imbalanced in our approach to life and not living from our true Nature. Rather, we are lacking a sensitivity to our various options and lacking a certainty about our talents.

On the spiritual path, we are concerned with perceptions about our uniqueness and surrounded with visions of past lives in order to determine our personal process of becoming aligned. The inner voice is a tool for our self-analysis.

We *sense* the inner *voice* more often than "hear" it. We *feel* the counsel as *gut level intuition,* which is the *voice* in a different part of our consciousness. When you first become aware of your whole being, you may not identify exact words or ideas. You may perceive inner pictures or flashes of color; or you may have a spontaneous impression of an action that will bring you success or happiness or give you a more definitive portrait of your destiny. Such perceptions come from your higher Nature expressing in a form that will help you best understand the information being directed to you for your whole need.

The inner voice is natural. Everyone has it and can learn to allow the inner voice and attune to it. When you are able to hear the inner voice, you are capable of surrendering to your better Nature, because you are then being receptive to the counsel of your soul consciousness.

The inner voice is our link to being divine. It is our connection with the higher planes of reality and to the personal Counselor many name God or Savior. The inner voice is not a personal process of thinking. It is only very delicately heard when we are silent in our thoughts. The inner voice is a technique of the whole Self for bringing insight and understanding into the consciousness of the physical self. More correctly, it is the voice of the Eternal Self.

When you are able to hear the inner voice's counsel as definitive concepts and words in your mind, you are becoming *still* enough to receive clearly. When you are able to be quiet within, you can hear the thoughts spoken *into* your mind. This is a tool of exact discipline and means you are releasing inhibitions and restraints upon your spirit.

The voice of our higher Nature speaks in a clear and distinct *thought* pattern. However, the voice is not audible; that is another kind of phenomenon. The voice of the supreme consciousness is subtle and soft.

We learn to hear the inner voice by taking a few minutes every day in *quiet time,* a method for learning how to become inwardly still. By attuning every day, preferably on rising in the morning, we train ourselves to hear this *still, small inner voice* that speaks softly. By such a daily discipline, we become attuned enough to shut out distractions and sounds whenever we meditate. This does require a steadfast dedication, because the process is personal and no other person truly can teach it to us. Others can only instruct us on how, but only we can actually *hear* the voice that speaks inside our own mind.

The supreme consciousness of our being *is* the aspect of the Divine that is always interested in what will bring us happiness and peace of mind. You can indeed attain inner clarity to the degree that everything becomes crystal clear in your perception of reality.

We learn to trust and to accept the advice of the Inner Counselor. The inner voice comes into our consciousness through our willingness to accept the responsibilities that come with being sincere in our devotion, fully realized in our talents, and a quality example of higher thought while in the body. The inner voice that you begin to understand is your higher thoughts spoken *into* your consciousness by the Self called soul.

The inner voice is a natural gift to us from the Creator to help us become our inherent Character. The inner voice is your most sacred Self giving you instructions and encouragement. The inner voice is a friend. When you first become aware of this process, you can depend upon the facts given to you—because they will support your evolution into being more helpful to yourself.

~ ~ ~

The first stage of being aligned and *hearing* soul's advice begins slowly. At first, the attunement comes in a state of unconsciousness, such as during a repast or contemplation when you are seeking counsel, such as through prayer. At first, you may not understand that, when hearing a word or a few words or ideas, you are being given advice that is holy and private and not supernatural but is your inherent divine Self inspiring you to raise your perception of reality.

The inner voice is the Counselor to whom we turn when we are in need of direction and support in our human struggles. The inner voice is discerned by realizing it is not a conscious process of analyzing. Answers come in *response* to our evaluations and questions. The inner voice *responds*.

At first, the distinction between the inner voice and your own thoughts may be vague. Yet the inner voice does become incredibly clear and accurate with your devoted attention to being available to receiving its guidance. By practicing a form of silence—any method of meditation—you can gradually learn to perceive what is being said and gradually increase in your capacity to hearing the inner voice.

The inner voice is always present to assist us. Before we learn to hear and heed the inner voice, we are not receptive or we discount what we hear. However, once we begin to trust that we are, indeed, hearing divine messages, we are ready to unfold into our life's purpose.

Let's do an exercise. Evaluate your experience *now* of hearing a thought spoken *into* your mind. *Pause and listen.* ......

~ ~ ~

Now reflect on how familiar this process *felt* to you. Did it feel natural or difficult? Do you find yourself willing to try the advice you heard, or are you arguing with your inner voice and denying the suggestions given? This tells you something about where you are in the process of integrating your soul power.

During the first stage of hearing the inner voice, we are learning to accept it as a guide, to accept its counsel and learn of our particular talents and the aspects of our Self so that we may be all it is our instinctive Nature to be.

The inner voice is pleasant. It is always gentle, never condemning or sarcastic. The inner voice is always kind and fair. It does not require of us *any* behavior that would cause us or any other person or creature pain or suffering; except perhaps changes in our personal habits, such as dietary recommendations and suggestions for improved social behaviors. The inner voice may encourage actions you don't prefer, yet you realize the truthfulness of the ideas because they feel familiar to you.

Important note: The inner voice also does not ask us to say anything to any other person. We are not asked to disturb any other person's life. In the first stage, we are not asked in any way to advise others. When beginning in higher-consciousness development, the only advice we receive from the inner voice is to enable us personally to become more whole—physically, mentally, and emotionally.

Any advice other than this is not the sure and sound advice of the soul. Any advice given from our soul is for our own development. We are not to help others until we have healed own discordant nature, says the Divine Mind. We are of help to others only once we ourselves are centered and self-assured.

Linking with your inner voice is for your own personal growth. Acknowledging your inner voice's counsel, and acting upon it with confidence and devotion, substantially enhances the process of your soul integration into your personality.

You sense the value of the insights, acknowledge them intuitively, and surmise that only holy perceptions are being offered. You realize that nothing is being given to you that demonstrates wrong thought or that might cause you to be misguided or to hurt yourself or any other.

Your only task—during this first stage—is to heal yourself of your own discordant behaviors, attitudes, and beliefs. Any other advice is judgment from the ego or that part of the self that is unclear. Punishment and retribution do not come from our soul, or spirit. Suffering comes only from the unclear aspects of our ego, or personality. Our higher Nature does not inflict confusion or pain upon us. We do it to ourselves.

If you are beginning the path of self-realization, perhaps this section is sufficient to help you identify and understand the inner voice.

Counselors of the Other Realms

Second Stage of the Inner Voice Perception

Once we have attained a personal level of commitment to be all we can be, by daily devoting ourselves to developing as a spiritual being, we begin to receive communication from *other* realms of reality, which also are given inside our mind.

We learn, over time, to discern our own processes of higher advice from information suggested by beings from other dimensions who communicate telepathically. The voices of the personal Counselors of the other realms are Ascended Teachers, angels, and correspondents in the various dimensions that parallel our own dimension. Those beings, with whom we can dialogue mentally, exist in realities as real as our own Earth. The only difference generally is that they are more advanced regarding how to evolve spiritually. Therefore, they advise and suggest particular strategies that will enable us to be more aware of our own personal destiny.

Ascended Master Teachers do sometimes supervise our individual functions. Eventually, they give us a universal understanding about life itself. During this second stage, however, they merely give us further instructions: to understand our personal purpose in life, ways to be selfless, and ways to live by the laws of life in every aspect of our being, including relationships.

The Ascended Teachers who assist us may be aspects of the Divine Self from which we originally came. They also may be our own Self evolved.

Other *intelligences* communicate in this same way. The consciousness of a being who is of a different perspective than ourselves is identified by its unique presentation of ideas and/or unique way of expressing itself. Each thought process represents an original and distinct personality, separate from our own, even those who are aspects of our own original Identity (the monadic being from which our oversoul extended). However, most of the *intelligences* who speak to humans are entities of a different degree of evolution than earthlings. In most cases, if they approach us, it is because we have reached an ability to receive a greater variety of communication.

The determining factor of our being able to conceptualize in this manner is our dutiful pursuit of higher consciousness. It is advantageous to be open to—in a sense invite—the presence of such Teachers when they wish to make contact with us in this way.

They are often available even when we are not aware of their presence around us or we do not hear them. We learn to perceive their sensitive presences of outer consciousness thinking *into* our mind. We learn to ascend mentally into the realms of thought wherein these Teachers approach us and send mental projections *into* our consciousness.

The many, many levels of vibration make it very challenging in the beginning to learn to distinguish among the various kinds of external communications and to identify the source or personality of each contact. When beginning the path, we may *feel* such insights more often than hear them. Once we are quite used to the process, potentially we are able to discern the difference between our own analyzing, dissecting, and identifying courses of action, from an *outer* being of light who is guiding us.

Important note: Unless you are definitely involved in a level of service commitment to humanity, it is very unlikely that you are receiving contact from a being who is more evolved than you are.

It *is* possible to hear information from less-evolved beings, and this is a vulnerability of aspirants studying esoteric techniques. So when beginning the inner path, we are cautiously advised to accept only our own Higher Self's insights—which you can recognize because they feel natural and synonymous with your own sense of who you are, and they resonate in your *heart.*

Even though at this second stage we receive direct communication from Teachers and angels who work personally with us on the inner planes, we are still asked not to counsel others . . . because we are still healing and attaining our own growth. The instructions we receive are to help us realize what is still unclear in us or that is restricting us from integrating as a divine Self. Even if you believe you are being given information, it is still not for others to hear, it is only for you.

We receive second-stage contact once we are definitely committed to being of *service* to humanity in some way. The determining factor is that we are committed in a deeper, more soulful way than ever before in our life. We are interested not only in our own evolution or spiritual clarity. We wish to be a part of the healing process of others. *Then* higher intelligent beings may communicate to us various lessons and training. In others words, we are tutored in the styles of being that are the laws of life that bring happiness and joy.

The Teachers offer their devotion, insight, and instruction. They counsel us regarding our personal activities, behaviors, attitudes, and beliefs. They teach us how to heal and release confusion and misunderstanding about our own personal truth. They give us personal counsel only when it will clarify what we need to know in order to accomplish particular tasks we may be given.

It is very important to be emotionally and mentally stable. It is wise not to assume prematurely that you are being guided in any particular action. More often, that is a delusion of the lower self. Only when practiced in this technique for a considerable time are we attuned enough to understand the nature of such a communication.

~ ~ ~

To reiterate, *during the first stage,* listen to the inner voice for support and counsel but not for advice on actions that would cause you or any other grief, disrupt your life, or dramatically affect anyone. The inner voice is personal. The inner voice does not control. The inner voice does not ask us to demonstrate our presence or power over any other person *or* to alleviate their worries. The inner voice does not encourage us to be elite or greater or supreme over any other person or creature. When new on the soul path, the inner voice is *our* own personal healer of thoughts and emotions. It does not give advice that will affect any other person's life or process of becoming.

During the second stage—once you are certain (without a doubt) that you are on the soul path, and you are disciplining yourself in a daily commitment to being of service—you can expect communication from the Teachers. At the same time, even then, you are still becoming familiar with the inner voice technique. You are still learning to refine the process of telepathic communication from other realms.

Until we clearly understand the difference among the various "speakers," we are very carefully tutored in how to be divinely inspired. Even at the second stage, we are still learning. Therefore, we are advised *not* to go into the world or to intervene in other people's realities. Instead, we are directed only regarding how to enhance our own process. We may receive very specific directions, but not advice regarding actions that will affect any other person. We are only given ways to become complete in our own multidimensional Nature.

In the beginning of awakening to our soul consciousness, we are not able to discern the voices that might intend disruption of our inner linking to The Thought. So if you are new on the path, it is wise to assume that you are receiving instructions for your own peaceful evolution . . . in this most *natural* way available. It is wise to assume that, even if you are contacted by other beings, they are of a higher vibrational nature and are training you in ways to be whole.

Once we are able to accept the instruction of Ascended Teachers and other able Counselors, we can see that their counsel is quite uniquely different from that of our Higher Self. Their manner of speaking, the inflection of their perceived tones, the inflections of their perceived ideas all vary according to who is speaking.

The process, of course, is *telepathic*. These beings are real entities who exist in other worlds, realms, and/or dimensions. They previously have been incarnate and are now in other planes of existence. They have evolved beyond the level of physical third dimension, although they are generally still aware of the physical state. Sometimes it is true that a Master or Teacher may not be from *our* universe, but that is less common. Of course, the beings we call angels have never been incarnate. They are present, because we all have personal guardians and counselors in the angelic realms whose sole purpose and functions are to serve humanity.

If you believe that you have begun to receive instructions from Teachers, remember that their advice is continuously in harmony with *your* own dedication to *your* process of self-healing. As long as we are attuning to our spiritual Self and seeking that most clear connection possible with our own divine Nature, we receive instructions from the beings who guide us on the inner planes.

During those occasions when we are not able to maintain attention or hold the focus, the inner voice can seem unavailable. However, it is not because the Counselors no longer support us. It is not because they will not return or are not present. It is because—in that moment—we are not at a high enough energy focus to comprehend their presence or advice.

How can you lift your vibration? Attend to the spiritual being you are. The more focused you are on developing and integrating the higher qualities of your Self, the higher is your vibration.

Our vibrational frequency as a living being continuously increases. We are various forms of density: energy, vibration, frequency. All things solid are various degrees of energy, vibration, and frequency. As we use our mental capacity, we begin to rise in our comprehension of the finer realms, which we perceive through thought, sometimes through images or pictures, sometimes through intuition or feelings. Images are useful as long as we can interpret them through our *inner knowing*. Intuition is useful as long as we allow ourselves to accept and trust what we realize intuitively.

However, although there are many ways to resonate with the frequencies of the Teachers, the most useful is to be clear enough that you can hear their actual communications in a language easily comprehended: thoughts and words *into* your mind.

At the second stage of becoming, you are still attuning to your sacred Self. You are still focusing all of your attention on your own process. Only once we have begun to truly heal, are we able to venture beyond ourselves—in a sacred way—to healing others and assisting them with their traumas, by way of our own inner connection and contact with the inner voice.

Beginning to Serve Others

Third Stage of the Inner Voice Perception

Once we have attained inner certainty as a loving being, as well as a level of commitment that surpasses personal need and desire (and only then, says the Divine Mind) do we begin to receive particular directions from our Spirit Teachers regarding functions we may provide to others.

Again, the Teachers and Counselors do not ask us to harm ourselves or any other. If this should ever take place with you, be warned: It is not the voice of a Teacher and you are not ready; you are still learning. Slow down, be patient, and heal yourself first. Until we have healed our own mind, we cannot truly help any other.

However, if you do feel totally aligned and centered in calm reason, without emotional involvement and without a need to prove your value to anyone, perhaps you are ready for the level of service commitment wherein you may receive guided directions as to your particular path of service, of which they are many.

It is vital here to describe the quality of the human psyche that indicates such a readiness so that you will not prematurely indulge yourself with the notion that somehow you are more advanced than you are. This is a serious topic because a few people have gone awry. They failed to listen to the light and, as a result, hurt not only themselves but many others.

The *inner knowing self* counsels us on how to be well, whole, and loving. How can you know if you are receiving clear information that will in any way affect another person's reality? What is the state of mind when beginning to perceive your Inner Counselor?

- *You feel inclined to discover your purpose in life.*

  You want to contribute in some way, although you may not know how. You want to assist others, to alleviate their suffering. How can you help them? First, heal yourself—your own wounds, your own psychic scars. It is imperative, in fact, says the Divine Mind.

- *You are seeking advice.*

  You know you are beginning. You are confused. You are reluctant. You are unsure. You are an aspirant.

- *Whether you admit it to yourself or not . . .*

  You are afraid of what might happen if you accept the counsel. *Know this:* Nothing you are asked to do by the inner voice will harm you or any other. It is not the way. You are given advice only to benefit your own physical being, your emotional being, and your mental being.

• *Very important:*

Do nothing that will cause grief to you or any other person or creature. The voice of conscience is a good friend and does not lead us astray.

It is good to be feeling the pull of your soul's counsel. The presence of Spirit Teachers indicates that you are beginning to move out of the personal point of view into the *impersonal*. But that is still only a beginning of your commitment to others. So, in the early stages of contact with other beings, remember this: You are just beginning. Learning is gradual. You are being taught how to be a whole person and how to love, when it is beneficial to share and when it is not, when it is wise to speak and when to keep silent, how much to divulge and how much to share, with whom and how often.

We *learn* to be helpers to the Teachers. They will, in time, work with you and through you (if you wish) but not until you have made sufficient progress in healing your own suffering.

When we are seeking to help others in order to alleviate our own disagreeable discomforts, we are still an aspirant. It is a good place to be, it is an attribute, but it is still personal desire. The process of helping others begins with helping ourselves first. We do not see clearly for others until we see clearly for ourselves. This takes practice. That is why it is essential that, when sincere in your determined commitments, you attune *every* day to the higher energies—to learn to be still and, in time, acquire clarity.

Many people on the planet are able to bring you more quickly into alignment, various teachers who channel and/or heal the body or spirit through various modalities, all of which may be beneficial. Your personal preferences, which you can discern intuitively, determine the path to take at this time.

~ ~ ~

At the third stage of the inner voice attunement, we are becoming more sincere, more level-headed, and more logical. At the same time, we are open and receptive to higher thought. We are calm. We are rational. We do not display emotions (other than joy, tranquility, and sometimes the overflow of soul in our heart). We do not get a rush of ego (power trips). We help others by first being emotionally and mentally conscious. We know we have healed our own pain (to a great degree), and we are ready to go to *the next level of serving others.*

In the third stage of the attunement, we begin to be of greater use to all. We begin to realize our innate perfection . . . and we are more self-confident. We have healed many of our personal discrepancies, of which we are very aware. We know our strengths and our weaknesses. We know how much we have accomplished and how much we have yet to improve. We are absolutely certain of our innate Character. We have a good sense of perspective of our whole Self, and we definitely have made a strong connection with our soul. Our communication with our soul is clear, strong, definite, and continuous. Therefore, we yearn to be of use in the world, in some way to help others grow into their own soulful Selves and/or help them alleviate their suffering.

Since we are now completely devoted and willing to be of service, our Master Teacher (member of the Spiritual Hierarchy) begins to ask of us particular tasks that go beyond healing ourselves. We are committed to being a servant of the light and a servant to humanity. Therefore, our personality is more sound and balanced, less confused and less obscure. That's when we begin to receive not only personal instructions but insights we may share with others, as suggested to us by the inner guidance.

Once we attain this higher level of communication, we have absolved guilt and regret. We have forgiven ourselves for our mistakes, past and present. We have forgiven others who have hurt us in any way. We may not understand all of these things completely yet, but we have synergized our spiritual Nature to a sufficient degree that we are no longer controlled by such emotions and beliefs. We have learned to let them go. We have learned the value of the spiritual planes of existence, and we sincerely hope to be of use in the healing and "becoming" of others.

At the third stage, when we reach out to others, it is not because of our own desire or need for recognition. We do not seek acknowledgment or acceptance. We do not help others because we want power or control. We do not help them because we desire to be seen as a good person. We have absolved and released all of these needs in our process. We have reached a point in our personal growth that we are free of these emotional constraints. We are free of the need to be loved. We simply exist in the presence of the Divine . . . and we enjoy that Company. We exist with a genuine compassion for beings of all natures—humans, animals, and otherwise. We no longer seek to fulfill our own emptiness. Rather, we seek to be a vehicle of Spirit in whatever ways we are guided from within.

Once we attain this level of service (when our heart is full of the spirit of the Divine) we are clear enough to receive instructions and requests of us to share with others our learning, experience, and measure of wisdom. We then become a servant of the light in a true way.

Conclusion

The inner knowing process has many stages. These first three stages of hearing the inner voice are the most essential to understand when we are beginning the soul path. Once we reach the third stage, we have attained a sufficient acclimation of understanding to proceed on our own. It is only during these first three stages that we are the least clear and the most vulnerable to self-deception.

These warnings are given not to hold you back, but to balance your perspective so that you do not make false assumptions about the process you are experiencing; because it is very typical in the beginning to be elated and inflated. It is common to rush out prematurely, proffering advice when we know not of what we speak.

The inner voice is a personal tool initially and is not meant to be shared with others until we have healed our own pain, to a great degree—and only we know when that time has come for us. These three stages are essentially the preliminary levels of the inner voice connection. As you attain the more fine degrees of this attunement, you will understand what the next levels are and when you have reached each level.

When we are able to accept ourselves as we are, with all of the various components of being human and, at the same time, rise into our spiritual Nature, we are then ready to be instructed by the Teachers. This does not, however, deny the significance of our soul. Soul is our essential link to the universe. Soul *is* our individual aspect of God. We simply can become more of the divine Self we identify as soul.

Learning to hear the inner voice is a necessary training when on the soul path. The Divine Mind encourages that we take time each day to commune in the *silence*—any form of meditation that helps you tap into the essential nature of the Divine, wherein you can perceive your own vast essential Self and hear the Divine guiding you.

We are all healers. We are all counselors. Once we release obsessing over our own personal dilemmas, our desires and emotions no longer rule us. We are able to rise above them and seek—with equanimity—whatever contribution we can make to ease the suffering of others.

The inner voice is with you now, already guiding you. If you do not yet hear it, *feel* its presence in your *heart*. Feel the *knowing* within you.

16

Your Comprehension and Perceptions Expanding

Imagine that you are now beginning to receive the Cosmic Teachers in your awakening process, to realize that indeed you are not alone; that They came before on many occasions to give you counsel but—until now—you were not able to fully accept the information divulged to you.

Once we have integrated the initial stages of self-healing, we begin to embrace the learned understanding given by Ascended Teachers. Once we integrate the various aspects of our whole Self, we become a person who is, in essence, our soul on Earth. In fact, we become imbued with the consciousness and attitudes of our soul.

This is most important to understand because, once we embrace the beliefs of our soul, and live those attitudes and beliefs, we experience Earth reality in a more harmonious and exploratory way. . . with a sense of *adventure.*

In the Earth journey as a soul-embodied Self, we increase in higher understanding to a defined point where we are able to distinguish between the usual strategies for self-realization and an improved strategy that comes through the expanding awareness of the soul-embodiment process. With an increased perception of what is holy and what is intuitively accurate, we are able to envision outcomes and circumstances unlike anything we ever before could understand.

In our expanded soul awareness, we are able to conceptualize differences between old analytical perspectives and the vibrant sensitivity of the Higher Awareness coming through our integrated, soul-embodied being.

Once we accept our new enlightenment as a person of hope and enjoyment of life, we become a teacher and a representative of the etheric Spiritual Hierarchy of the Ascended Masters. Once we accept an increased comprehension of the laws of nature and incorporate those laws—to the best of our ability—we become a presence of comparatively enlightened wisdom. We are *then* asked to shoulder some degree of responsibility in helping others in their development into this higher experience of living.

When we explore our consciousness, we find an unlimited capacity for intuitive reasoning and a clear understanding of life's mysteries—which heals our curiosity. We no longer strive to understand . . . because we have learned to access the archetypal memories of the human psyche as well as the universal insights— which are the same in all dimensions.

For this reason, we become exceptionally able to bring our inner conscience into our personal understanding of the many who are eager to comprehend something besides day-to-day existence. Reasonably accepting ourselves as a representative of the higher realities becomes essential because, by then, we perceive the evolutionary aspects of being.

Once we are ready to decide who we are, our full array of cosmic wisdom is already present in us. We have only to pull ourselves into that comprehensive anticipation and realization in order to access that Self completely. Once we do, we measurably shift from old importances and values to more heavenly interests; which primarily are duty to humanity and duty to humanity's elder brothers and sisters in the Spiritual Hierarchy.

Once we integrate this concept into our personality's needs, we have begun a completely different level of personal expansion in our own evolutionary process. This is a completely unanticipated level of experience because, until now, we have not really thought about becoming a teacher. Our intention has been to be more whole in our own framework of ideas and abilities, to express ourselves with greater ease.

We also have not imagined ourselves in the role of our being an *inner* counselor by way of thought projections *into* other people's supreme consciousnesses. However, indeed, this is exactly what we now begin; not because we choose to but because we are asked by the Spiritual Hierarchy to contribute to our earthly brothers and sisters who are also seeking to find the way.

We invoke cosmic abilities that, until this point in our soul development, have been dormant in our psyche. By accepting our precious intuition as a vehicle for our soul power, we open a variable and essential doorway into the inner kingdom from which come all wisdom and information, which now also have a greater use in our life than we ever imagined possible.

As we uncloak our visionary ability, we begin to realize a scope of personal insights about our destiny unlike we previously could access or appreciate intuitively. In fact, we become all we have sought to be . . and more.

Once we reach our inner kingdom—in its full splendor—we have survived a multitude of confusions and disappointments. We have accessed our personality's deepest and most foreboding crises and resolved these admirably, compared to our previous struggles. Since we have acquired a technique for our own good, we can now access cosmic consciousness—our divine Self—and illuminate various distortions in *other* peoples' psyches so that they, too, can be happier, more fulfilled, and enjoy the fruits of being human.

There are many advantages to being human, says the Divine Mind. However, until we acquire the inner vision and learn the laws of nature, we cannot understand the spectrum available through the human consciousness. Yet once we believe in our good Nature and invite the integral beliefs of our soul's consciousness, we are *beyond* any previous knowing, far beyond any imaginable kingdom of insight. Once we invoke cosmic awareness into our experiences, we invest all of our attention to that, and the universal dimensions of attitude become our own.

This is when we unconsciously invite the Inner Counselor to instill us with a yearning to be of use to others in some way. Our potential is to add our own input to the archetypal memories of which we now become a part.

The Universal Mind is a *living form* composed of the beliefs and values of Cosmic Teachers—those who are illumined from within by their own spiritual awareness. When this becomes *our* own experience, we too tap into The Mind in a fluid way, which is unstoppable and continuous and is more natural and accessible than we previously could imagine.

We then agree—in our inner place—to help humanity through our own comprehension of the universal teachings. In this way, we begin a higher level of our own evolutionary reasoning and we are infused with the potential of a "blended" consciousness.

Humanity as a whole is undergoing this expansion now. Humanity is reaching a comprehensive participation in its own evolution. The human psyche is expanding in its capacity to fulfill the higher presence of attention to planetary interactions and self-healing. This is now beginning to be apparent.

Once we accept our responsibility to each other, that is when we access the new revelations of higher thinking, invoke the higher ability to imagine a more harmonious way to live, and begin to appreciate others as spiritual beings.

Humanity is now upleveling in integrity to such a degree that nothing will dissuade the whole of us from becoming the natural human beings we always have been becoming. Once we as a whole have acquired the universal consciousness of goodwill toward all, we will be a higher conscious race. This is, in fact, humanity's destiny.

The world we have lived in, for most of Earth's history, is *now* upleveling its energy pattern into a higher vibrational frequency. This is changing our experiences very quickly. In the increasing frequency, everything is speeding up, including our process into higher awareness. This indicates humanity's readiness to ascend into our more substantial soul-embodied Identity.

Following is a message of praise from our brothers and sisters in the Spiritual Hierarchy. This inspired thought taps our innermost closeted place wherein we arrive at our own instinctual comprehension:

- *Believe in the potential, and it will become reality.*

- *Believe in the complete perfection, and it will be reality.*

- *Know that you are whole already, and you will be whole now.*

Once we become a voice of the higher teachings, we begin to live in the voiceless realms wherein the secrets of life are made clear. It is, in fact, natural that we come to this point of self-realization. We become aware of the Universal Laws in order to heal our own discordant behaviors and to invite the Universal Mind into our own.

The universal *intelligences* of life are many. As we invoke the higher knowledge of the archetypal memories, at the same time we are able to communicate with positive Teachers in all realms of existence. This is a natural extension of a developing consciousness. Once we truly begin to accept our own unique potential intelligence, we are receptive to the insights given by our Elder brothers and sisters.

The Cosmic Teachers invite us to hear their thoughts in our hearts. They are present. From many realities, they are coming to inspire us with their visions of hope . . . so that we will accept the new reality we are creating. These Teachers of cosmic understanding already have evolved beyond where we still are. They are bringing us understanding of the nature of life, because they have been through this same evolutionary process into the spiritual Self.

The Cosmic Teachers are coming to us in many different ways: through the inner voice, inspired sensitivity, imagination, and creative expression; even through manifested forms recognized by our outer physical senses. This latter method is receiving a great deal of media attention today. There is much taking place on the planet that is revelatory about these beings who are guiding our process of awakening to being whole.

In addition, the Teachers whom we call extraterrestrials are just as real as we are. In their own dimensional way, they too are valuable attributes of the universal wisdom. They, too, are coming to Earth because they have learned to utilize the full spectrum of personality integration with higher understanding. The natural process of comprehending their value will bring humanity into a full comradery with their participation in our planetary culture. Eventually, our communication with these beings will be friendly and without fear.

My friends, we are not alone.

17

The *Inner* World We Discover

Creating an outer reality that satisfies is the objective. A successful outer reality is steeped with the values of the *inner* society. So, let us now travel the inner world.

Imagine yourself in this plane of consciousness: You have a holistic outlook and point of view. You observe the natural bond between you and others. You respect the consciousness of all living animals, fowls, mammals, and humans; as well as beings of other dimensions, including angels, devas, nature spirits, gnomes, dwarfs, elves, sprites, terrestrials of the inner earth, and terrestrials of the fourth, fifth, sixth, and seventh dimensions of Earth.

You enjoy divine satisfaction with these pre-eminent travelers of the universe, who are humanity's ancestors and kin. You know these travelers; you honor them and acknowledge them. In the softer senses, you respect their different appearances. You accept their uniqueness. You sense the essential thread of sameness that binds us all. You live in the sure knowledge that none of us could exist if somehow all the others were destroyed.

In the *inner* world, we are receptive to the higher understanding of the Universal Laws. We live by the cosmic truths that give direction to all levels of creation. We believe in the strength of the Vital Force and we count it as essential and fundamental to all of life. In the limitless realm of our eternal and cosmic Self, we appreciate our unique place within this multidimensional society. We see that every person is a member of several planes of existence. We feel our relationship with many types of conscious creatures of the Universal Thought, and we live in harmony with them. We see them as instrumental aspects of the Total Divine Being. In this decision, we are unbounded and released from the torments of outer confusion.

Every person is a part of the inner society. It is the part of us that is the most vital. By living this essential Nature, we are drawn into the social exchanges of inner beliefs. We are surrounded and taught by illumined souls of the higher planes, such as angels and evolved spiritual beings from our own soul's lineage. With their guidance, we learn to more easily release the old attitudes that have ruled us, because we are most simpatico with the beings from whom we descended.

The realms of the inner kingdom are a comparatively unexplored frontier. By integrating and living our personal values, we bring our inner life into our experiences of the outer world. In this way, we are attesting to the inner life.

We are able to venture into this "land" of wisdom whenever we choose, to dialogue with other species, including other mammals, even to reach the stars without traversing the physical dimension.

If you could make this journey in an instant, would you go? Would you embrace the farthest reaches of your inner consciousness?

How can you know if the inner world is reality or fantasy? You find that your sense of *knowing* is all the surety you need.

When we are ready to explore the various levels of the reality of our soul, at some time we each come upon this inner society of creation, because the inner world is a part of the manifest world in which we live. The inner society is the kingdom of our true Identity—the Self we each *sense* we are.

During this journey of the inner pathway, we contact at least one other species of the inner society. In this way, we learn to believe in the greater truths of life, to remember that humanity is but one voice in the vast unknown and that there are many voices.

Part IV

The Turning Point

18

Moving Beyond Your Past

"The Turning Point"

When do we release the caricatures of ourselves? When do we move beyond the past? In esoteric wisdom, this is called *"The turning point."*

When we accept our new Identity with strength and absolute conviction and are no longer overcome by the people who have injured us in life, clarity and resolve fill us and actualize through our insights. We know who we are, and we no longer resist our soul power.

When we relinquish the fear of being unloved and we embrace our ideal Self as our true Nature, we go forward in life as if reborn. The Universal Consciousness imbues us with self-appreciation and forgiveness of others' mistakes against us.

For me, *the turning point* occurred in the summer of 1994 while attending a family reunion in Austin, Texas. For the first time, I accepted myself as I am, rather than the way others had believed I should be or thought I was. I began to realize that self-acceptance is an essential step toward developing personal consciousness.

For all of my youth, I had allowed myself to be controlled by well-meaning relatives who had influenced my life choices. I had allowed their past voices still in my mind to control me. Needing approval had been my prison. Nevertheless, being rebellious—seeking my own inner *drummer*—I had struggled against the expectations of society.

After that reunion, life for me was different. My oversoul had "reparented" me over the years since 1975 and given me the love I felt

I had missed; and the Inner Counselors had shown me the way to accept myself. They had given me a clear point of view and something in me had resolved itself. A new identity was now present. I no longer felt controlled by my fears or self-doubt. I still had fear. I just no longer let it control me. I found the courage to move through it and beyond it.

We learn to love ourselves, and we learn to accept others as they are. We learn to open our heart and follow our *inner knowing*. We learn to accept life as it unfolds (seldom according to our plan). Once we recognize our commitment to spiritualizing our life, that is *our* turning point.

19

Humanity's "Turning Point"

The *turning point* is a primary stage in our personal soul evolution. It is also esoterically a group initiation for the entire human race.

The spiritual path—awakening the soul consciousness—reaches beyond personal development. Self-realization becomes more than finding peace in our own heart and mind.

Once our heart is awakened, we feel the need to live with honor and integrity, and we make actions that count. We feel the need to reach out and help others. Once our heart is awakened, we yearn to live for more than ourselves alone, because we recognize that all of us are in this world together, that what *we* do counts, what *we* do matters.

How we live affects everyone else. Everything we do and say impacts everyone around us. Our desires and thoughts become our words and actions. Our beliefs are visible on our face, in our gestures, in our tone of voice. We are not invisible. Everyone can see and feel who we are. The purpose of the soul path is to free our compassionate heart, because the compassionate heart heals all. Once we have accepted the responsibility to live the best we can as a spiritual being, making choices for the highest good of all, we affect the whole world positively.

The whole of humanity is affected by each person who releases into his or her soul expansion. When we lift ourselves, we lift the world . . . and we become a part of a world transforming. When we are kind, patient, tolerant, and forgiving, that tone vibrates out around us as potently as a stone thrown into a pond, rippling waves out around it. The ripple effect goes on and on and on to the ends of the earth. Living consciously (making conscious choices, thinking and behaving thoughtfully) is the transforming factor that ultimately will change the world.

We are now in the process of becoming more able to be what we were born to be. Nations all over the world are expanding in their desire for autonomy and personal freedom. People are striving to understand how to live in this world as our hearts dictate. It is not an easy task. Yet, says the Divine Mind, inevitably we will learn. The conflicts, ruptures, pain, and suffering are a way of dissolving our old beliefs . . . and discovering our compassion.

In society today, we are beginning to see the potential for self-realization (spiritualization, for which we were originally created, says the Divine Mind). With each person who adapts to the soul consciousness, more and more the whole will be affected.

It is easy to look at all of our problems and be discouraged. It is easy to see all that is wrong with the world. Yet it is important to also see what is right . . . and to keep our vision high. Humans have a tendency to rise above their circumstances. We shall again.

We have the benefit of history, and we have the technology to bridge the communication gulfs between us. All that is left is learning compassion. Compassion brings people together. Compassion opens doors, minds, and hearts. Compassion is the tool to heal our social wounds and our misgivings.

A revolution of concepts is now unfolding this wisdom . . . which will heal our social and cultural misconceptions of what freedom is and what happiness is. Humanity is unleashing its spirituality. We are no longer uninformed. We are able now to live consciously.

Our personal consciousness is our spiritual Identity. Our personal consciousness is who we are as an integrated, whole individual. Consciousness—a constantly evolving web of vitality—is the *texture* of our true human nature and is the *body* of God.

As you and I and every other person awaken to our soul—in heart, mind and body—we feel emboldened to rise above our limitations and to help others. We discover that life is bigger than our personal troubles, that life is about *service*.

The soul path is a personal journey. It is also a journey we are making together. Each life is important. Each matters. Understanding our place in the whole can free us to build our own dreams and to fulfill our own vision. Understanding who we all are as a people can free us as a society.

To understand the big picture, following is an overview of how humanity began and where we are headed.

20

Our First Leap of Consciousness
to Homo Sapiens

Before we were human, we were angels—illuminated beings of light. When we became human, eventually we came to embrace the false belief that we are limited. True sight, hearing, insight, and intuition were veiled to us. We lost the ability to appraise situations accurately. Our faculties were imprisoned in the illusion of the new form and we were unable to surmise the truth about any occurrence.

So when the opportunity arose to alleviate our density and increase our true Nature, we were delighted. We had struggled in physical density for a long, long time before we enjoyed the burst of inspiration called *"Awakening."*

This was humanity's *first initiation* into a higher conscious state of knowing, which alleviated our then even more dense emotional atmosphere than we know now. It seemed like a miracle! For the first time in what must have seemed to us an eon, we were able to perceive once again the possibility of our innate Nature: the angels we had been.

The *still-clear angels* gave us this burst of inspiration, this tool for higher recognition. They trained us to conceptualize a more blissful existence, which was our hope, because physical density was heavy, our minds were dull, and we sensed we could be more.

Over time, we grew more sensitive. Eventually, we began to dream about *The Before Time* when we had been pure and free, when we had enjoyed the full delight of our blessedness. As we dreamed, we did not realize we actually were remembering. Nevertheless, our imagination expanded the part of us that is divine. We viewed this as mysterious and magical.

Our ability to ponder and envision increased and we grew intelligent. We began to perceive elements of our being we had not before felt or known. During this time of expanding consciousness, we became safer in our emotions. We felt a strength and power that surpassed our reason. This mesmerized us, fascinated us. At least most of us. Some early humans were afraid. That is when we first knew the ignorance of superstition, when those who feared the soul power called it *"of the dark."*

Those of us who knew that the soul power is divine, embraced it. We soaked it into our full awaking selves. We were hungry for wisdom, and the inner power gave us wisdom. We were thirsty for peace and tranquility and, in the fullness of the power, we were tranquil. We longed to be acceptable in our own eyes; and, in the depth of the power, we knew our whole Nature, which was glorious, and we remembered our divine origin.

As we became more and more attuned to the new selves into which we were evolving, we grew confident. We grew in our capacity to conceptualize. We became increasingly more endowed with the inner mind, increasingly more open to our whole potential. Those of us who totally released to the soul power evolved into a different kind of being. We left that dense physical body behind us like a shell out of which we escaped. We lifted in a new physical body of more energy and more decisive insight.

In the new human body, we extrapolated solutions much more clearly, and we determined strategies previously unimaginable. In the new human body, we were able to fulfill our grandest hopes, to fathom expectations never before thought, and to grasp certain potentialities never before conceived. In the new human body, we were closer to being the divine Selves we once had been.

This leap in our being was the birth of the human being we are today. Even though we may forget we are this creature of grand and wondrous delight, all of us on Earth *are* this human being.

When we strive toward the light, angels of light surround us and hold us up. In numbers innumerable, these divine beings of light give us hope that moves us forward, delight that reminds us of our true Nature, inspiration that stretches us into our wondrous Self. The angels of light release us from the depths of our sorrows and release us from forgetfulness. They are always with us.

As the second generation of humans, we began in this world—Earth—as homo sapiens. That is when we became truly human. Before, we were lost—lost in self-deceit, self-gratification, and self-delusion. As real human beings, we were, for the first time, able to perceive our greater Selves. We could imagine our whole potential. When we each began to actually support ourselves in this new vision, we continued to expand in our consciousness.

Some of us embraced the glorious. Those who did evolved beyond the state of being that you and I know here today on Earth. They saw their true Identities as divine beings. They absorbed their full imagination, embraced their full capability, and ascended into their more clear light. They became *"The ones in the light."*

Today, those elevated beings of light are still with us. They are the voices of goodness. They encourage, teach, and help us to realize that we, too, can ascend beyond the beings we currently are. We, too, can become clearly illuminated Selves, as they did.

We feel their presences around us as delicately as dew drops upon rose petals. Their consciousnesses pervade our senses. Their reflections fill our imaginings. Their wisps of breath are the thoughts that speak within us. These beings of light are round about us in numbers without limit. They hold us up to view our true potential. "We are your brothers," they say to us. "We are your sisters. Come. Join us. Let us once again attend to happiness."

These Enlightened Ones who are no longer physical teach us through our minds and hearts. They counsel us within to guide us into peace. Their ideas are as fresh today as millenniums ago. Their words are as substantial for healing our lives as millenniums ago. Even more so. Embracing the teachings of these spiritual Masters shows us how to reconstruct the boundaries by which we live. Studying their ancient knowledge and devotions shows us how to live wisely.

Human life is an evolutionary journey. Humanity is not a stagnant race. We are consciousness—in a form of our own creation, by our thoughts and by our beliefs.

As we think more truly as our spiritual Self, we clear our body of the densities of the third dimension. We lift into the realm of beauty that is our true Nature.

As we heal our false ideas of what is possible, we find ourselves increasingly more able to be the angelic presence we once were.

As we more and more invoke our true Nature, we begin to live it every day.

As we practice, so we become.

21

Humanity Is on the Brink

Humanity's Awakening

My friends, humanity is becoming light. The human race is evolving.

As we uphold our virtues, we raise our insight into the finer dimensions of expression. As we uphold our goodness, we increase our energy frequency into a more aligned presence of our natural state of being. As we uphold our fairness, we lift into being what we have always felt we could be: our potential fulfilled. As we uphold our kindness, we ascend into our higher level of being.

Humanity is elevating *now,* as a whole, into that higher realm of being. We are ascending into our greater Selves. As a whole, we are reaching our more illumined presences. This is a new *"awakening,"* the second only since humanity began.

We are stretching out of the womb of mass human thought, breaking through the resistance of false humility and false concepts of power.

This *second awakening* is carrying us from a limited way of being into a new way of seeing ourselves, each other, and our world: to accept each other the way we are.

Once we have completely passed through this transition, however long it takes, as a society we will have become spiritualized human beings. We see evidence of this transformation by looking within our own hearts. We are each aspiring to be more than we have been. So are all, and there is much to be hopeful about.

Ideas and beliefs shape the world we live in. We cannot escape our beliefs, but we can transcend them. We can grow. We have before. We will again. We are already.

We survived the Dark Ages. We went through one Renaissance in the 1600s. We are now going through another.

Humanity is on the brink of rebirth. We are on the brink of *the turning point*. Once again we will lift into a clearer presence of our light.

While all about us life seems discordant and in disarray, we today walk in a world becoming free of the past. The transition from what we have been to what we will be is the struggle to make sense of things that can no longer be pigeon-holed.

There are no easy or simple answers. The journey is difficult because we are striving to find our way through uncharted waters. We have not been here before. We have not done this before. Learning a new way of being is a massive challenge. However, humans have always lived up to challenge. We must remain confident and hopeful and continue to do as our hearts lead us.

The journey to soul awareness is not easy. It is life changing. Living as your spiritual Self is a constant juggling act to remain centered and balanced.

The great effect, however, is simply *bliss*. You like yourself, believe in yourself, forgive yourself, and forget yourself.

As you release to this heart expansion, you ascend into trust and peace—and become all you were born to be.

Revealed Teachings

Volume II
Your Personal Transformation

Part I

Invoking Your Serenity, Which Is Your Inner Strength

Be assured, your personal insight is expanding. You are fully able, now, to embrace the visionary you. The end of confusion can be yours, now, when you uplift yourself in the inner stillness.

The universal counselors merely remind us that it is our own inner light that shows us the way. Our own inner Self is already absorbing the instincts of the Wisdom. Our own inner Self is ready to enable the full aptitude of our serenity.

For when we immerse ourselves into the deepest inner place in our being, we are filled with a serene and calm *knowing,* which is already in us. When we immerse into our most sensitive inner quiet, we feel a deepest release. We let go. We feel the humming of our own core vibration and, in this, are nurtured. For our whole Self is a living Us that already functions fully to guide us.

Your whole Self *is,* now, awakening. Open yourself to breathe into the serenity. Breathe it in. This is where all healing is born. This is where all understanding is attuned: in the deep resonance of your whole Self, inside you. Be allowing. Be uplifted. Be in your own essential Nature. *Breathe.* This is who you are.

Today, the world hums. Feel the world's humming vibration. Feel your own humming vibration. All that you have sought, the feeling for which you hunger, is in this inner resonance, within you. Feel the stillness. Feel the deepest, deepest releasing, now.

And so here you are ... in your deepest, deepest release. You are here now.

You, too, are a healer. You are now able to heal your pain. Let it go. It is not the full you. In this way, resonate. In this way, uplift yourself. In this way, you are fully here—all of you. Be your whole Self and know:

> *"My life is today.*
> *I am grateful.*
> *I am aware.*
> *I am all that I have always been.*
>
> *No more fear.*
> *Only absolute understanding.*
> *Now, I know.*
> *I know who I am.*
> *I am in my own strength.*
> *I am in my own serenity.*
> *And this frees me.*
>
> *I am now fully free.*
> *I am here.*
> *I am."*

Your More Tolerant Self, This Is the Blessing

You are opening to a more aligned connection to the Divine. This is already within you. Now it is expanding.

This is the effect: You are more tolerant (meaning forgiving) of situations that test you. You are more able to let go of harboring discontent. You are more easily convinced of your own misperceptions, thus accepting that others are just as wishful as you for fulfillment and meaning. You now better understand the inner self of others, feeling their intention and desire to be happier.

These teach you more tolerance. So that you are slower to judge and condemn. So that you are more controlled in your thoughts, and less often and less harshly lash out, if only to yourself.

This personal expansion in you is an upgrade in your whole being, for it is more the Self you are without the shadows of everyday anguish. It is more the Self you are without the heaviness that has anchored you in disappointment. It is more the Self you are without the human expectation of repercussions.

In this lighter Self, you more easily understand how being full in your heart is healing. So, now you seek to live with a full heart.

The way to feel full of blessedness is to open your feelings to the caretaking of others. You begin to reach out beyond yourself to those who are inundated by sorrow and are lost in despair. By opening your whole feelings, you begin to live from a place not only of nurturing but also wisdom. For the giving Self is one who is able to become more attuned to the harmonies of all life. In this, wisdom blossoms in you.

So, this hour, release and let go of all you have wished for. Let go of what must be. Lift up your anticipation of a more insightful you now blossoming.

Your new Self is born in a grateful heart. Be glad for all that is yours and in your life. Release all disappointment—and only breathe in the next moment, which is the Divine living in you.

In this, you are now set upon a greater possibility. In this, you are full of peace. In this, life is now more wondrous.

The Ageless Self

You may wonder how you look to others.

As you look at your reflection in the mirror, when you believe you are light and essentially divine, you see in the mirror the reflection of your true Nature. You see your glow. You see love.

Only the body ages. Even that can be kept well for generations. When we integrate the breath of life, the power of *All That Is,* into our being, our focus clears. We are confident. We are calm. Through practicing the ageless wisdoms, we learn to realize that the true experience in life is through the divine inner Self.

We humans are essentially kind and considerate beings. These are the aspects of our inner Self. The radiating glow of our essential Self transforms our physical body until it becomes an ageless and vibrant vehicle.

We also become more aware of and sensitized to the loveliness and grandeur of physical life. We appreciate the potential peace of the planet. As we bring the Life Force into us from the ethers, we begin to realize that life is what we make it, that our emotional feelings and physical health generate the quality of our life.

So when we open our heart in our profession, in our relationships, and in our creative process, that is when we *feel* our divine essential Self. That is when we become what we wish to be.

When we find the divine within us, we are filled with strength. The frailties that we imagine are not our true Nature. We are everything we dream and imagine we can be. We have only to act on this to discover it in our life.

Your Presence in the World

Suppose you could remove all of your inner resistance? If you could rebuild the world and be a power in the world, would you?

We have the exceptional task of rebuilding the world. Are you intrigued?

You are essential to the rebuilding of human society. For all of life is a reflection of the state of consciousness of the whole. It is the natural state of humanity to resist. That is the prevalent state. But when we have acquired self-awareness, we are able to help recreate the world.

The forces of nature are energy, and mind is energy. One influences the other. When the predominant thoughts on the planet are self-consciousness, the result is a society of ill-shaped dreams and that society is a reflection of ill-mannered people.

It is the powerful and essential presence of self-aware, enlightened people who pull up the energy of the united mind.

There is, at present, an enormous resistance toward a better world. This is because the influence of enlightened ones is getting stronger. It is the mental presence of these humans that is effecting a more socially acceptable environment.

Those of the Eternal Flame have the sensitive task of rebuilding society, because they are aware of the ability to do so. They are not asleep. They have evolved out of the oppressive self into a Self who illuminates all.

Dear friend, as an illuminated person on the Earth, you can help restructure the very foundations of thought.

How can you cause society to redefine its priorities? How can you affect society's beliefs? How can you influence individuals into acquiring self-analysis?

Since the earliest and vaguest moments of human consciousness, there have been beings of greater wisdom whose mental prowess has caused the human population to expand in its ability to think at a higher level. Such beings have always affected the whole of humanity, by their continuous and ever-present commitment to raise the vibration of thought.

It is this consciousness that those on Earth who have attained a measure of insight can similarly relate.

As we gain more presence, we also gain more influence and affect the overall tone of the human vibration.

So, to be of real use in the world, seek to raise your own level of consciousness. As you become more aware of the cosmic planes, you are also more aware of the fullness of life. When you are endeavoring to bring this awareness into the human process of behaviors, you can be sure that the effect is present. Although you may not readily observe changes in people's demeanors, you can most certainly expect that those changes are taking place.

Keep in mind that all of your personal choices affect the whole. Knowing this causes you to strive toward being more centered, because from that center you can be the clearest and most rational self possible. From your *center*, you can observe all of your own discordant emotions and all of your discordant patterns of thought.

From your center, you heal your inconsistencies and learn to be your true Self, who is gentle and wise.

Our natural state of being is this enlightened Self. When we apply ourselves to developing this attitude, and when we anticipate this result, then indeed that is what we become, for what we desire and expect is what we later become.

Our beliefs shape us. Our beliefs shape our actions. Our beliefs shape our experience of the world. When we are able to cleanse our beliefs of the distorted views and expectations that plague most of humanity, we are beginning to raise our perception of life. We are then able to facilitate positive results in our own being.

Can you imagine how you wish to be? Can you be filled with unparalleled tenderness, increasing sensitivity, increasing goodness? Can you be your whole Self fully present?

Not only can you effectively heal your own worries, you can help heal the worries that plague the whole. For it is the spiral influence that is always effecting change.

By re-estimating your beliefs and values, and healing and forgiving your pain, you are becoming an influence of good in the consciousness of humanity.

Be Innovative

To get above diminished prospects and economic opportunities, take a position of confidence.

The individual mindset is able to totally restore opportunity. Think through alternatives. Envision other ways to meet your needs.

Why sit by and wait when you yourself can feel and foresee the trends in value? Imagine *your* contribution. Believe in your own vision. The solution is creative problem-solving.

Why accept defeat? Why give up? Why wait for someone else to tell you what to do? Be innovative. Make your own answers.

Dream. Build. Act.

You are your own solution.

Aligning to Your Whole Self

When you are in sync by intention, it is like putting into your attitudes and yearnings a deeper connection to *That Which Is* the central vortex.

A *Living Mind* permeates *every* atom throughout everything. Just as on Earth the tides affect the seas and the shores and all within and upon them, so the alignments of stars and planets are as these tides because all of space is *not* a vacuum. It is not merely a void, or like the air around you. It is more like an ocean, essentially with the quality more fluid-like. So that all of these "movements" have a causative effect (a ripple effect) upon everything else.

Now, because Mind is the essential quality of *all that is,* when you set your focus with an intention, you are more in the alignment by your will rather than it merely impacting you. Either way, you are affected; just as tides on the Earth (by sea or by land, as in earthquakes; by air, as in air currents), your life and body are impacted. Yet when you *focus* an intention, mentally, you are in sync with the tides (whatever their source).

As a result, your mental attunement (even your physical attunement) can become crystalline in its clarity, like the perfect clear note of a bell's harmony resonating from a single "RING" out and out and out. You, in essence, become by intention *The Resonance.* It's like the perfect tone humming outward and outward and outward. This sets *through* you such a synchronicity with the Fullness of your being that you touch God, in all of life. You feel it in you. You know.

Accepting the Divinity in Yourself

We do not think of ourselves as being perfect. We think of ourselves as becoming divine only once we have died and gone to heaven. We forget that heaven is what we make of life by the way we live and by the way we accept who we are.

Our religions have given us guidelines for how to be perfect. We accept them as allies to align us with the Source.

Perhaps we can learn from Teachers who have gone before us. They have come to show us that we can be complete in our *present* reality.

However, we do not have to depend on Others to show us the way. The light of soul breathes in us, and all thought is available to us from the Cosmic Mind.

The great Masters have led us toward this regeneration. They are our bloodline to God.

We are learning that God is the divine within us, the illuminated one within us, and that we can access this true and complete Self.

This good fortune results from raising our social consciousness beyond the sordid problems of the world:

> *"I believe in myself.*
> *I believe in the power of the universe.*
> *I believe that God is within me, and that*
> *I am able to transcend my pettiness and my fears,*
> *to cooperate in making this earth into my heaven."*

You As a Self Have Always Been

Life exists to perpetuate the divinity of the cosmos, which is a Mind and what is called universe, space, void, the nothing. God is a Presence, an effervescent life substance that Thinks.

This Energy Essence has always been. It is. It is the Texture of the vast reaches of matter. It is the glue of the vast elements of the Void.

All that exists is this life. It is the very construct. It is the nature of the cosmos, all dimensions, all layers of perception, all depth and breadth. All that exists is this Existential Force, which has been and will be any and all Thought. So that, before life, It Was.

You began in this Void also, before life. As a part of this Ocean, called Thought, you have always been. You have existed since the Mind's Expression. You existed before any universes. You existed before galaxies. You, as a Self, have existed since *The Always* thought you. You have existed, as a Self, since *before* any physical depth. You have existed always in *The Bliss*. You have always been. You will always be.

Life as a human is in this Long History, the history that began before worlds came to be, the history that began when The Mind brought Selves into consciousness. You have been since The Mind thought you, as a Self.

You then, as now, were consciousness. Consciousness is the substance of who you are. Consciousness exists outside and beyond the brain. Consciousness is the stuff of *what is*.

You are always aware. You are always expanding. You are always becoming, to be all you can Imagine *is* life. And that is why you are here. To be.

So, Imagine a better world. Because what you imagine is the world you live in. Imagine the world as it can be, and that is the world that is being birthed, now. Life is you.

Your Transformation

Let's look at individual transformation. The process is a breaking down of old ways and systems, in order to make way for a new way of being.

Each of us now on the planet is undergoing transformation in some way, to some degree—and this is more than the typical growth experience. The energy of transformation has increased and is being fortified in *our* time. There is a fretful energy about us. Many people are confused. Many are seeking clarity and direction. Many don't know what to do. This is part of the process. Accepting that the process can be enlightening, even joyful, frees us from the pressures we feel.

Transformation begins at the personal level. The transformation of us as a people is the evolution of the human species. Our lives are altering in many ways. We are increasing in awareness. We are becoming more compassionate. We are learning to care for others besides ourselves. The old barriers to human interaction are breaking down. The old ways of thinking and patterns of belief that have limited our abundance are changing.

To personally transform, first allow new thoughts to come into you. Then extinguish/disintegrate beliefs of injustice and dissatisfaction, which are seeds of failure and are self-annihilating. Bridge from an old way of being to the new—by self-love.

When we accept, self-forgive and experience spiritual release, we express this to others as well. When we allow ourselves to be interdependent, we find peace in this changing world.

Nothing is constant. We expand beyond faults and temptations through an inner constancy of courage, self-discipline, new thoughts and feelings. Feelings of unreality, failure, and incompleteness fall away. Old patterns clear out. Newness roots within. Out of this newness blossoms our new Identity: the whole creative Self.

Self-love and love of others enables us to transform without being overwhelmed by the life changes themselves. Think of your personal transformation as a flower emerging. The seed of full potential is within you. To reach your full potential Self, nurture the new attitudes and ideas within you.

Each of us is becoming a fully actualized human being. We are becoming what we are meant to be: the Creative Force expressed.

Your Enhanced Self Begins Now

Now begins a new cycle of personal consciousness. Now begins a lifetime of increased personal insight.

Now begins humanity's revelations about its own actions. Now begins the heart awakening of the human species.

Until now, humanity comparatively has walked as if in a dream. Now the veil lifts. All becomes bright. All is seen. All is felt. All is realized.

This is a healing, for it raises expectations. It increases perceptions. It shines gentleness into hard hearts. It opens psychic scars, that forgiveness may fill the wounds and renew the happiness that was once in you.

Now begins your heightened insights. Now you come into your next senses, which are an expanded range. Now you feel a caring coming more fully into you, releasing all quandary. Now you release. Now you can be at ease. *Breathe.*

This is the beginning of the enhanced human. This is, for you, an increased understanding of your own fullness ... so that it is more easily entered, embraced, and lived.

To enhance yourself, find the inner quiet each day and breathe in it.

Breath is the way. Breath instills your full and true gentle Self.

The Time for You Is Now

All born since 1970 have a clearer connection to the inner self. This has the result of clear knowing and also the inner wisdom of the spiritual realms.

You are, therefore, awakening yourself, because you feel the incredible life presence in you and understand that life is upgrading now.

Your life, now, is difficult at times. You have had sorrows and unexpected upheavals. Even so, know this: Now is the beginning of your full being. The time is here. It is now. There is no more waiting.

You are, now, fully able to step out and give all that is in your understanding. Be not afraid. Be happy. For your deepest anticipation is now unfolding.

Part II

WE Are All an OCEAN of Life Presence: One Being, One Breath

Life is evolving in every way, at this time.

Lift your insight through the practice of **Deep Being**. This is sitting quietly every day, allowing your Full Self to enter you. You feel complete. You feel restored. You feel like you are tapping into the cosmic forces. *You are.*

When you are open to your lighter Self, you feel nurtured. You feel complete—as if your breath, deeply in you, is aligning you with the entire life forces. *It is.*

All you have to do is be. Be in each easy breath. Simply feel it. The secret is simply to focus and consciously experience this breath. It is the natural *pulse* of the *Whole Presence*.

This is who you really are. In your Deep Being, you are in a gentle sense of: *Here I am. Here is everything. Here is all. There is nothing else.*

This is the center of you. This is how you renew your body, expand your mind, and illuminate your essential Self.

In this place, you hear the angels. In this place, all knowledge comes to you—because *now* is **The Expansion**.

We are simply a threshold away.

Breathe now. Simply be. Feel the Universal Essence moving in you.

All is a **living breath**. This is life, the pulse of all.

Do you feel it? It is quiet. It is steady—you and *all* around you, both seen and unseen.

Life is continuing continuously, always and ever. Feel it?

This is how all are one. A continuous, single, essential breath. Life is one breath. All are one breath. That is what *The All* is.

Now, let go. You are in this constant soup. Feel it?

This is how *all* are one, a single fabric, and every moment in this experience you can feel:

> *"This is life.*
> *Everywhere.*
> *We are all this gentle breath,*
> *as if we are one being,*
> *as if the very air around us is what binds us.*
> *Everything is this living life."*

Be. All are one: one being, one breath, bound by a single *ocean of being*.

This is life: a single pulse, one breath. That is how we are not separate. We are each a living cell in an ocean of cells, a *drop* in the **ocean of being**.

When you feel it, then you know that therein is how all of life affects the other, because we are all a part of this ocean of being. Like fish in a stream, we are in it together. That is how we feel connected. That is how we connect. That is why everyone's movement shifts our lives.

You, Now

Life really is all about being able to feel a direction and glean an insight. The more aligned you are in your own Breath, the finer the *inner link* to the perceptions of wisdom.

The whole capacity to fully integrate is yours *now*. Therefore, hold yourself in the fullness of your total presence. Invoke your whole Self and breathe into that strength. It is who you already are. You have only to breathe it in.

We Are the Society

In generations to come, people will still be talking about their problems. However, as a people, we forget that we make our own reality.

If life is not flowing for us properly, there is something we aren't understanding about ourselves. When we don't believe in harmony, we create disharmony.

Too often we encourage in ourselves disruptive behaviors. We resist being happy. We resist allowing peace. We are ready to fight at a moment's notice when things don't go our way, rather than look at our own behavior and seek a way to resolve the experience.

What kind of cooperative effort can we bring for an amenable solution for everyone, and take responsibility for our own dilemmas rather than blame society?

Society's ills are our ills. Our attitudes create the society we live in. When we appreciate others, rather than fear or resent them, they appreciate us. This has a cumulative effect on the racial consciousness of the whole.

Let's look at one significant area in life: how much money is coming in from your job.

The job may not be exciting or nurturing. It may provide only a paycheck. If that's true, it's necessary to look more closely at that job. There is more reason for being there than the money. Other experiences are making the job worthwhile, probably one or more persons you work with.

What is that person getting out of your presence? Is that person becoming a more clear being by your interaction? What are you getting out of the relationship? What are you discovering about yourself by your interaction with that person? Did you know you felt that way?

There are many kinds of personal growth experiences. A job is one way we grow. Life is a series of experiences that we create and allow in order to observe what kind of human being we are; to observe our behaviors, attitudes and beliefs, and how we handle stress and discord and whether we make friends.

These are aspects of being human. A job is a structure through which we discover ourselves. When we appreciate a job for its true purpose, the money becomes secondary.

Life offers a multitude of experiences for accepting our essential and true Self. When we flow in our natural serenity, anything can happen ... *and* we can still remain centered and not become disoriented, angry, or bitter. We look at situations for what they are. We can take responsibility for our emotional and mental confusions. And we can let go.

How we handle personal stress and the dire straits of life is reflected in society. Society reflects all of us; and all of us interacting are affected by the whole.

A peaceful society begins with self. We dialogue lovingly. We accept personal responsibility for our personal growth. We are self-disciplined. The way we dialogue sets the stage for what our society is.

Therefore, by clarifying ourselves—mentally, emotionally, spiritually, physically—we can affect the whole. We can influence the direction in which society is evolving. We can manifest the kind of world we want.

How to Maintain Inner Stability

Today represents a massive marker in humanity's evolu-tion. The hour is in flux. The critical resonance is a wave of ideas, a wave of new ways to see options, a wave of enormous new discoveries.

The decade ahead bodes change, more confusion, less stability, emotional flushes, and temperamental spurts. It also opens and releases calloused fears, with the fresh breath of exposure. Individuals are stricken by honesty. There is a leveling. Perceptions now shift to include an entirely new vision. Hope heals.

Yes, it is turmoil. Yes, it is aggrandizement. Yes, it is more uncertainty. It is also softer expectations, more resilience, keener visualization, precious forgiveness. Old wounds open. This is difficult but a necessary cleansing. Then there is a rekindling, a cautious levity.

By addressing the emotional chaos, the earth's pulses will gradually stop convulsing. This era is hard. It is challenging. It requires stamina. It requests patience.

Believe in yourself. There, find equanimity. There, hear harmony. There, be instilled with insight. There, feel direction.

As the global shifts perpetuate and societies are pushed, forced, to alter their means of functioning: Find your own kindness, to remain in your patient disposition. Find your own generosity, to foster well-being and gentleness. Find your own resourcefulness, to keep your life situations serving your needs. Find the equanimity of your own resolve. Find the assurance of your nurtured conscience.

Find your compassion, and all the social convulsions will not shatter you. Find stability by invoking *that* vibration down into your body and mind. As you invoke this soothing recognition of your whole Self, stability fills you. It is inborn. It is an inner vibration. Stability is inside you.

No rush. Steady, now. Calm, now.

The unhinged world is not your world. Watch it. See it. Observe it—from within your *stillpoint*. Steady, now.

This is you: Confident knowing. This is you: On your own self, calm.

The Economy and How You Can Help Yourself

The United States will recover its financial presence, but "it takes another presidential term; not because of who is president, but because of the public doubt. The United States population hovers in discouragement." Yet both the U.S. and Europe will regain their ability to care for their people.[2]

The economic downfall is not an accident. It resulted from greed. Whenever one does not consider his or her effects upon others, it affects everyone. The lessons in this are compassion, integrity, discernment, and humility. The lesson is: Do not throw everything to

---

2 Received September 2011.

the wind but be exacting in measuring the repercussions of blitheful actions. Whenever others' needs are thwarted with disregard, to the exception of the self who is more bent on acquiring favor, the result can be catastrophic.

This economic fiasco in the global cultures is an opportunity to reinforce perceptions about the use and strategies of power and institutions. Whenever anyone abuses his or her influence to the gross negligence of the whole, there will be a harsh repercussion.

So what is the solution? Meet your own obligations. Be fair. Do not disregard others' personal circumstances, if your choices will elevate you to the sacrifice of all else.

Here is the answer: Anyone who uses his or her power and imagination solely to collect glory will lose everything, in particular the calm heart that brings contentment. Anyone who flaunts, with disregard, his or her imagination as only meant to bolster self's successes and riches will be destroyed, in life and in the mind. One cannot treat others with disdain without the consequences being harsh against all, including the self.

Thus, what can you do? Honor those who depend on you. Keep your word.

This economic crisis was "mid-stream" in September 2011. We can get past it. It will correct itself—once the fear begins to more gently dissolve. All the anger and fury have caused such a critical backlash in the western psyche that an entire generation's lives have been altered forever.

The generation of graduates — twenty- and thirty-year-olds — sees the results of economic blackmail as a harsh lesson in humility. This is like a scar in those whose hopes have been lost. At the same time, it *resets* the healing attitude that life is not about self alone, but that everyone is part of the common good.

The result of this emotional *reset* is an entire generation who are more likely to move in attitude toward thinking of the whole. This attitude is what heals the rancor. For until there is a preponderance of such change in actions, the downslide will not yet be stopped. In the western world, all are still teetering on a precipice of cataclysmic downturn.

Now, the good news. You as an individual can overcome the economic losses by building your own vision—from a heart filled with a yearning to be fair. You have an insight that is new, imaginative, and prosperous for all. *You* have not only an idea, you have the resolve and the heart to give back to your society, for the good of all. *This* is the attitude that will shift the economic trend, from aggrandizing to sharing. For a nation that thinks of others is a nation that rekindles its lost faith.

The western world has forgotten how hard life was for its great grandparents. There has now been a wake-up call. One cannot abuse others without destroying the very foundation of society. Society can only work when the greater number understand that everyone is a part of a whole. As long as abuses of power are tolerated, everyone suffers.

The years 2011-2014 were a period of recapturing dreams, getting back to hope.

To do this, as a nation, it is critical to realize: the nation is a composite. It is everyone. As long as more than the few succumb to feeling there is no recourse, there isn't.

But as long as you, personally, begin to change how you live in the world, with others, toward others, for others—the national despair will begin to heal.

America is not finished. But we are on the brink. Will we choose self-glory over the needs of the weak and uneducated? Or will we use our imaginations and hearts to be contributors? Will we take and take and take, giving nothing in return? Or will we use our imaginations to invent remedies, to find solutions, for the common good?

For a nation is not its government. It is its people.

Tyrants and Bullies

The universe has a way of balancing the scales. Foremost, any who harms another is destroyed in the mind, suffers a lack of calm, agonizes while flaunting success. Any who harms another is punished by the law of cause and effect, a natural cosmic force that means whatever emotion/energy is projected returns a thousand-fold, in some form, into that person's life. There is always loss and devastation in the life of one who is cruel.

As the world is now *upgrading,* this factor multiplies yet again. So that, whatever attitudes, biases, and judgments are projected (through thought or action) they will come back upon that person as a tidal flood of destruction, in some form that to each person is felt as a catastrophic hardship. Until that person begins to realize the pain he or she is causing others, such forces of nature will attack that person's state of mind, destroying the ability to have any peace.

This is how we learn to be kind and humble. This is how we learn to apologize and forgive. This is how we learn that sometimes a vengeful attitude hurts us more than other persons.

This does not mean we must accept another's murderous rage or intent. Justice is not blind. It prevails. It is important to stand up against tyrants and bullies. It is important to be firm in your own truth, revolved in your own confidence. It is important to stop cruelty and injustice in all of its forms.

Simply know this: Life is our choices. We can live with a forgiving heart yet also stop all damage intended by others. Being forgiving does not mean allowing others to destroy. It means seeing a human being's true essence underneath the harsh actions.

Hurting others is borne from fear. When someone is vengeful, it creates a perpetual cycle that has no end. Whatever is thrown out *ripples* into all lives around us. This is why we are told, be kind.

Sometimes, however, it is necessary to bring another to justice, to stop the harm that a selfish aggrandizing personality is perpetrating upon others. Cruelty must never be accepted. It must always be stopped—but with a heart recognizing it is a necessary step and not done out of hatred. Judge another's actions only because that person is not a healthy member of the body of humanity.

Such actions must always be stopped. The wellness of the whole is always the foremost goal. The goodwill of the whole is the guiding principle. So that, anyone who is harmful by intention must be made to address this and not be allowed to continue such actions.

Stop all who harm others. It must be so. Because the whole is the greater good, because it is the whole that we all are.

Our Evolving Global Society

In this new millennium and new century, we are reappraising our lives. Thereby, society is transforming also. Let us look at what we are becoming.

1. We are a people unparalleled to any age before us.

We are creatively and socially learning how to build a habitable environment. We are focusing on healing what has been destroyed by the unthinking ages before us. We are concerned about the environment. We are seeding the new world and trying many new methods of redeveloping the planet. These methods include hydroponic gardening, which offers considerable vitality and long-range possibilities; plus replanting soils, trees, and plant life.

We are also restoring sacred sites of high energy potential. We are acknowledging the devic kingdoms for assistance in healing the planet. We are interested in the well-being of all species of animal life, both land and sea; in particular, the whale, which has been a subordinate species on our planet but is a kindred spirit on others. And we are arranging to redistribute food supplies, which gifts have been sociologically and politically abused.

2. We who appreciate the human condition find ourselves in a world overpopulated and ill with a multitude of diseases.

Therefore, another group of the new society that we are becoming is the healers of humanity. Psychological ills, emotional depressions, and physiological breakdowns are all prevalent on Earth. However, regardless of how much we may recognize this condition historically, it is significant to mention that the ills of our current global society are pronounced beyond any previous cultures. There will continue to be a rampage of such diseases until there has been a complete purging of our old ways of being.

Many people of all ages—men and women—are providing assistance to restructure our physical world and to harmonize our emotional society. This is a particularly more interesting provision than previously. Rather than curing what has plagued humanity, these people are helping to re-stabilize our psyches and our physical bodies. These people are healers. They heal our hearts and our spirits. En masse, these people are creating a new desire in our social consciousness.

As a result, humanity's consciousness is becoming substantially more aware of the desire for wellness in all forms. This affects not only our present population but those yet to be born, the new consciousnesses. For when a thought form rises to such a potential that we expect to be whole, that is when the thought becomes prevalent in all society.

Until that point in our social evolution, however, we need healers, because they transcend all previous knowledge about what it means to be physical. These healers ascend in heart awareness and move beyond previous mental limitations. They envision potential problems and resolve them. They are greatly sensitive to others' needs, and they have a clear understanding of wellness.

Therefore, our well-being as a human species is transforming. In time, we will see that the human body is itself structurally changing, both physically and emotionally. For now, we must realize that our bodies are clearing what has interfered with our full potential as entities of the God Force.

There are many individuals who will not follow-through on this healing in themselves. They will fall prey to the many passions that rule the Earth. However, a great number will, either consciously or unconsciously, follow their hidden desire to pursue Whole Self wellness. For that is our state of being in the new world.

3. New spiritual teachers of the planet carry an understanding of mind, heart, and being. They understand levels of consciousness besides the physical.

Consciousness is now stretching—for many of us—beyond the perimeters of known consciousness. People of many races and many doctrines are beginning to realize that we all speak of the same God. They are dropping the barriers among us, and they are rising to the opportunity to explore new forms of this *collective* experience. We can see this in the changing perceptions of the whole. Religious thought is being re-evaluated. An understanding of life's great mysteries is forming in our collective unconscious.

The people of this evolving new world are guiding us in appreciating ourselves and in releasing all distinctions between us and others. These teachers of a new way of being are messengers of light, sent forth from the angelic kingdom in an effort to remove the hindering energies of our old world. The combined effort of these teachers and the presence of divine thought will give direction to society's illness and healing. These teachers do not posture themselves as exemplary. They focus on lifting up others around them.

4. The animal kingdom is also evolving in its level of consciousness.

A number of species on Earth carry in their being the new focus of the evolving consciousness. Whales and dolphins are two such higher forms of consciousness. They are in transformation also and will continue to dominate the waters throughout the history of Earth. However, there will be a complementary reality between them and us. This will enhance communication with all species on Earth, and elsewhere.

In the coming times, as we on Earth move into this new focus, there will be—unparalleled in history—a communion of us humans with the creatures of the seas and of the lands, and of other worlds.

The door is opening for intergalactic travel, not only outward but in receiving. We will commune with many different forms of life who are choosing now to take Earth into the Confederation of Planets, now that we and the Earth are moving into a higher level of consciousness.

We are entering a new era of responsibility. As a member of the Confederation, we will be joining forces with many different societies. Even though we will shift out of our old forms of thought and belief, we will—for a time—nevertheless still be reflecting the histories of our peoples. Even with the new consciousness, we have much to do to correct our social memories and the hostilities we have born and repressed for countless centuries.

Members of the Intergalactic Council are ambassadors to Earth. Some are here now. Others will be here later; the specific focus of this latter group will be to instruct and re-teach the members who have been incarnate on the planet.

Our connection with beings of other life forms and with the Intergalactic Council is essential to the longevity of our Earth species. We continue with the cooperative effort of beings of the other kingdoms of life.

5. *While we may look elsewhere for our salvation, nevertheless the task of personal and social transformation is our own, individually.*

We may seek and search through many different places for understanding. We may read many books. We may go to many workshops. We may struggle greatly to let go of that which pains us. However, eventually, we will remember that we are all beings of the God Force and that we are not alone.

We become aware, at a point in the development of our sensitivity to life, that there are many other levels of consciousness than the one we are presently in.

We become aware of worlds beyond physical reality. As this happens, we see that life continues endlessly ... and has always been.

We learn to commune, through our hearts and with our feelings and in a language that is beyond explanation, with entities who are not physical but nonetheless are as alive as we are. These beings are masters of light who have been what we are, yet have evolved beyond us. Some have never been physical. As we seek the counsel of these beings of light, we learn to appreciate that we are all kindred spirits of the God Force.

We and Planet Earth are transcending. We are moving beyond what has been our nature. As we pass into this higher energy, we may be overwhelmed by personal decisions or personal disaster, for the energies are very real and are felt in our lives. We grow by letting go of the pain we have lived. We have much to discard: misconceptions of truth, perhaps people in our lives who pull us down, perhaps a life condition that is not the way we now wish to travel. So, we let them go.

Transformation is personal, even though it happens to every person on the planet, in one way or another. We can learn to move through our changes with grace and self-love. When we feel the touch of the Divine within, we realize it is all worth it. When we embrace the Divine in our attitudes and personal lifestyles, that is when we become a member of the new world.

Living As Your Intentional Self

Awaken, dear soul on Earth. You are not your body. You are your mind. You are not limited to physical senses. You are all that is your sensibilities. It is time to awaken to your full Self.

You are now finding your way back into the Fullness. In these many millennia, you have traveled to the stars and from the stars. You have been a Glorious Being and Earthling.

You can, increasingly, become more aware intellectually of all life and the formulas of goodness: how to live in joy, and how to feel your own special Identity, which your original Self, called soul, and is your eternal Identity.

You are always this knowing Self. In the world, it is forgotten. But, now, the veil is gone. There is no more forgetting. You can now come out of slumber and embrace your essential Self.

Why? What's the point? Because this is how you can understand: your true capacity, the qualities of all people, and the characteristics of what it means to be an Intentional Self.

You are coming out of the *Time of Forgetting*. You are sensitively opening yourself to a fuller and more content existence. Is this not what you want: to feel purpose, to feel your own compassion again, to care? Is this not the vacuum that has caused you to feel disconnected: the not remembering, the not feeling, the not understanding?

You can now open your consciousness to the Self you are, which is easier and more at peace. You do not, any longer, need to be in struggle. It can end today.

When you release your fear, you open. You then begin to remember the innocence, the simple happiness, the You who is always in tranquility.

In this, you can now simply pause, and breathe. For Insight is yours.

Earth Is the *Result* of Our Reality

Stabilizing self-discipline rearranges the inclination of dependence on outside controls and allows us to find a stronger sense of expectation from within.

Although it is often true that we do not really have control over our world situations; nevertheless, it is now suggested that this is no longer the only way to survive.

It is important to realize that consciousness is a force of the living God, and that this force can measurably change and rearrange any condition, whatsoever. The only limitation to altering our whole focus of life is our reluctance to follow such thought processes to their conclusion.

Often we have a feeling to do a certain thing; then later, upon analyzing our potential concern, decide it isn't something we want to

152

do. While such choices are always considered extremely necessary; nevertheless, this creates a dichotomy within us. For, if we were to stay with the original conception, very likely there would be true fulfillment.

You see, when we are fully able to allow an experience to develop, we are also allowing the full identity of our higher Self to develop.

Although consciousness is nonverbal and intangible, it is a viable source of power. Consciousness is an unlimited supply of ideas. It is also the way we receive new attitudes.

For example, suppose you are walking down a road and see a man talking to a tree? Do you determine that the man is not all there mentally? Or do you open the vision of your inner self and *look* at the tree?

You see, every living aspect of life is a form of consciousness. It makes little difference whether it takes the form of a man or a tree. Why do you think there are so many different kinds of animals?

Now, what is being suggested is that the time has come to stop pretending that our world, Earth, is a causative factor of our reality. For it is *not* the cause but is the *result*.

Earth is an example of our projected beliefs of what is real. If we were able to perceive a different Earth, the Earth would be different.

This is not only the individual's focus, however. It *does* involve the consciousness of the planet, which includes the humans on it.

However, what if those humans had a different belief? What if those humans were able to *see* that their world is not frozen or turbulent, that their world is not a prison, that their world is not a game; but that their world is an extraordinary opportunity to play with the forces of reality?

You see, Earth is not the diminutive impoverished source of agony that many perceive. *Earth is our experience.*

Now, why is this matter brought to our focus? Because the time of the limited concept of an Earth of suffering is ending. Although it may take a few hundred years to fully be acknowledged by the people on the Earth, nevertheless it is so. Earth is healing. So are the beings upon it.

My friends, what is being discussed here is a leap in the human race's consciousness, an explosion of consciousness, and this leap in consciousness brings even the species of humanity to a new focus of reality.

We are each now beginning to so alter our ideas of truth that we are opening ourselves up to new ways of being and we are becoming fourth-dimensional feeling creatures.

Through 2170

The new Cosmic Age commenced September 22, 2011 with the autumnal equinox, and lasts 26,500 years.

Through 2170 is the opening of the Insight through (1) the inner counsel and (2) the expanded serenity.

Even as you invite this inner connection, it is already resonating in you. So, be open to your own enhancement.

When you are open to your own higher senses, you recognize a slight expansion in your abilities to envision and imagine. You increasingly perceive with an enhanced comprehension, and it is as if you have done this before. It's still you, only more perceptual and more insightful into the dynamics of the people around you.

Increasingly, this expanded attribute reveals to you a more attuned capacity to feel your own future. This is the natural ability to perceive the direction in which you are moving. You become more easily able to perceive outcomes.

This enhanced ability to perceive helps you begin altering fear-based actions toward choices based on the direction your soul is guiding you.

This is a turning point for you. This is the new Age, the new cosmic age.

Is Spirituality the Religion of the Future?

Now, we are awaking to the inner promptings of our souls, and this is becoming a necessary part of our lives. Indeed, this is now expanding in the personal awareness of a larger number of humanity than ever before.

We are also now being given higher instructions from a number of Ascended Masters who reside in the finer planes of reality. The Masters can, indeed, bring into our awareness principles of being that illuminate strategies of how to live in harmony.

The Masters have been with us all along; but we, for the most part, have not known this. We have been so engrossed in our own little worries that we previously ignored the consciousness of the world's Counselors.

These Teachers of the Spiritual Hierarchy can now reach us in ways never before available. For we can now interact with them at a level of attunement not possible in the human consciousness at any previous time.

This means the human mind has become more receptive to the ideas and thoughts of the realms of angelic beings and other higher forms of conscious life.

This means that we on Earth have evolved greatly in the last four centuries. We have even explicated our understandings with a percentage of craziness. For all of us, who indeed understand, are accessing mind canals that previously were not universally available.

The greater number of sightings and inner-voice linkings indicates the changing consciousness of the human race. While it may seem as if we have always been able to hear that voice, it is now much easier than ever before.

The reason for this is that the veil is now gone (with the onset of the new cosmic age September 22, 2011; in the 1980s, the veil was dissipating).

The veil that has blocked our view of reality has been disintegrating for several decades. In the last six decades (prior to January 2012), humanity began to access its group consciousness in a more sensitive area, which means becoming a voice of spiritual demeanor.[3]

It is time, my friends, to realize that we *are* evolving—even now—into a more conscious people; that we have become so inured with our understanding of the capabilities of a spiritual being that we are now realizing our personal link with those realms.

This, then, opened the door for all means of being spiritual. The universal wisdoms are available to every human being. There is no longer a need for intermediaries. There is no longer a need for ministers to describe the conditions that have been considered holier than "normal reality."

We have arrived. Humanity has evolved, sufficiently—even now—to restore our link with the Cosmic Mind of God. We no longer require special intercessions through another person. We each must, in fact, learn to become attuned to the spiritual worlds. For it is in this that we realize our own goodness and our power and that no one else can direct our spiritual flowering. Only we can.

Therefore, there is a profound impact on the social structures of humanity, because religions have been the foundation of human society since humans began to think as a higher form of life.

The normal evolutionary process has been to give our power over to another. The next step of the spiritual journey—now—is to keep our power in our own heart and become aware—ourselves—of God's guidance for us.

The impact of this on the world's religions becomes an implementation of change. Crumbling about us are the delusions of power and grandeur of those particular forms of religious institutions that have grown slumberingly upon the backs of others.

Now those foundations are disintegrating, because they have been built upon the sorrow and weakness of others. It is time for these institutions to dissolve. It is time for these institutions to evacuate their spiritual sisters and brothers into society, where those who were

3 For numerous discussions on the "veil is now gone" as well as on the new cosmic age, read *The New Humans*.

previously cloaked by their own false humilities now will become one of the masses.

In this way, the individual person in the world must seek self-empowerment. For there is no intercessor to speak for us to God. There no longer can be. For the veil has dissipated and is no longer a separating force from higher awareness for the masses, to anyone. While not all people have accessed this yet consciously, it is nevertheless becoming a norm by which all of humanity will live, in time.

So, the numbers of us who do already perceive this possibility are expanding exponentially, day by day. And the day will soon arrive, within our lifetime, when it will become the prominent focus of our being to be spiritual and to have a spiritual outlook on how we live, with each other. This is truly a turning point in attitudes. It also represents a crisis for those who have steeped themselves in religiosity rather than in the spirit of God that imbues the heart, mind, and soul of each person.

How does this transition take place? It begins in the unfolding of Spirit in those who have previously worshipped themselves as intercessors of God and humanity. They themselves begin to see and feel the change of consciousness. This already has taken place and is currently in the process of expanding as a necessary evolution of spiritual thought on Earth.

The transition, therefore, of the structures is already in stride—and nothing can stop it. For the outcome will be a complete collapse of all religious forms that restrict the personal connection with the divine being.

Can we personally exercise judgment against those who desire control? No, we cannot—for they are us. Just because a person has followed a particular pattern of thought or religious form does not mean that person hasn't been seeking God. In fact, the shift of focus from outer forms to the inner consciousness for these persons will be more challenging than for those of us who have not felt the restrictions of behavior, attitude, or demeanor by any particular dogma. Those who have abided by their dogmas their entire lives, or are steeped within them, will have a more difficult time of releasing to the spirit of God than those of us who feel the presence of God, already, in our hearts.

So, rather than be harsh with their perspectives of reality, they need our compassion and they need our support. They will find, within themselves, the foundations of their social structures crumbling. It crumbles from within. It is not an outer force that destroys an institution. It is an inner force expanding outward, from within, that destroys the need for an institution. Therefore, the institution falls.

So, indeed, we do see that religious thought is altering, and that the way in which we unify through the religious form is altering. And nothing can stop it.

Now, the spiritual Teachers of Light are awakening the hearts of the many to the inner Self. As we ourselves grow in spiritual alignment with the forces of nature, we become imbued with the presence of the Masters who counsel and guide humanity.

It is this impact and shift of perspective on what is religion that alters humanity's experience. In fact, we are, for the first time, realizing that we are truly divine beings. With the help of the numerous spiritual teachers on the planet, those who are wise counselors and fair judges, we are going to continue unfolding on the inner planes within our own beings.

This is a process of healing our pasts, healing our wounds, forgiving ourselves and others, and opening our minds and hearts to the new strengths and insights within us. Therein lies the victory of spirit. Therein lies the foundation of the new religion—which is not a form but is a way of life.

At the heart of all religions is a spiritual truth. Upon those truths may we rebuild together.

Religious writings are translations of the Universal Mind. When we read from our heart rather than our mind, we sense the essence of a truth given. It is the essence that binds us. For we all live by the same essential truth: the *Oneness*.

All religions have a glimpse of the truth. They are all translations. They were all taken through human channels. So when you read religious writings, read from your heart rather than your mind. Touch into the writing through what speaks to your feelings (your spirit).

Your ideas and what you relate to are going to change and expand throughout your life. Your perceptions are going to alter. You are going to become aware of different things at different times. So, just have an open mind and open view and relate to what speaks to you at that point.

This does not necessarily mean discarding or discounting other people's interpretations; but just see it as their own interpretation.

The Catholic Church had its origins in an ancient mystical society. It has now taken on form, as others have. The form is what is breaking down. The traditional approach is what is breaking down.

What you want to go for is the basic *qualities* behind the form, behind the tradition—to the *original concepts*.

So approach religion from your heart, from your spirit. If a religion or its concepts fit, use them. If they don't, don't. That's really all that matters.

In this new Cosmic Age that we are now in, humanity will realize that God is within; that God is a force that permeates all existence and is intelligence and consciousness; and that humanity is an aspect of that Energy, that Force, that Consciousness.

The church is you. It is Spirit working through you that is the spiritual experience.

There are some basic rules to live by. The golden rule is a good one.

As long as you feel you are doing your best, that is really all that is expected of you. And you are the only one who can define what your best is.

Being on a spiritual path is not necessarily being part of a religion—though a study of world religions does show us the similarities in spiritual thought; as do newer writings from philosophers, visionaries, mystics, and spiritual teachers.

Evolving into a Higher Vibrational Being

We have looked at what pulls us out of hope. Now, it is time to demonstrate humanity's power.

The Spiritual Hierarchy of Planet Earth sends to us the rays of life that transmute our innate power. These rays are the source of our enhancing awareness.

As we consciously choose the condition of our body—physical, emotional, mental, spiritual—we receive instructions from our soul as to how to be in the world. We are given enlightened knowledge about how we may contribute to erasing the chaotic patterns of our emotionally stimulating experiences. We are refined physically so that our body is more highly attuned than we imagined it could be. We are encouraged to strengthen our will by adopting new patterns of thought.

The reason for reinforcing our *light body*—which is integrated into the very membrane of our physical body—is to synthesize and track our psychological patterns in relationships. The Cosmic Teachers encourage us to daily synergize our body with the planetary grid system so that we may realize how we are the epitome of that grid system.

Our body—the consciousness of our being integrated in a physical form—represents a vortex of interdimensional communication powers; which also, simultaneously, synergizes with the universal forces.

Exercise to Reconstitute Your Body and Consciousness into Your Higher Being

The following exercise restructures our body and consciousness into the higher vibration.

Once or twice daily, focus your intention through your body, simultaneously toward the earth and to above your crown.

Imagine yourself sitting within a vibrating force. Feel the energy whirling upward, spiraling continuously in waves through your body, increasing in vibration until you feel the constant steady flow of movement in every cell of your being, so that you *become* a beam of power that is radiating outward, continuously.

Now, dissipate all magnetic frequencies from your being. While radiating your vibration outward, see yourself eliminating all negativity from your psyche and physical being. Dilute and dissolve these.

Now, breathe.

Now, bring in—as through a funnel—the bathing, healing resources of total discernment, well-being, and creative force.

When you feel full, bring your vibrating force back in and seal it within you, so that it bursts vibrantly through every cell of your body, through every pore, activating the original intent of your consciousness.

Now, stretch out horizontally on the floor. Spread your limbs outward in a star shape. Pull in the power of the life force. Drink it in through your heart. Visualize it generating outward circularly, throughout your limbs. Visualize the life force demagnetizing the mineral contents of your body, wherein are the deposits of the crystallized formations of negativities of all your past experiences and beliefs.

Now, sit up. Keep your spine straight. Feel the life force penetrating your spinal column, head to toe. Feel yourself linked to the earth and to the powers of life around you.

Exercises such as this immediately reconstitute the body. With that comes an ability to conceptualize new thoughts. This enables you to receive inner counsel about your own existence and the way you interact with your environment.

The Masters of the Spiritual Hierarchy await the opportunity to link you with their frequency and connect you with the Source Light.

Revealed Teachings

Appendices

The Messenger's Awakening

The Divine Presence exuded through every cell of my being, nurturing every thought, attitude, and emotion. I had come out of a long inner darkness and a month of unexpected awakened intuitive abilities.

It was Sunday, November 2, 1975, two a.m. I was thirty years old, divorced, and living alone in my apartment in Colorado Springs, Colorado.

In the middle of this long dark night, a spontaneous mystical activation into cosmic consciousness shattered my self-image and transformed my sense of self, as if I had been picked up and set in the opposite direction.

My outpouring heart opened me to all the wisdom of the ages streaming into my consciousness. I poured myself wholly into the fullness of this new divine and ecstatic place of human beingness, and a tremendous euphoria filled me. I felt the grandeur of the Universal Consciousness—of which I then *knew* I was an integral part. For the first time, I had a sense of identity and a sense of purpose.

An irrepressible explosion of insight and wisdom whirled through me, transforming my small sense of self into something profound and larger. The world was suddenly filled with vibrant sounds, textures, images, and colors. Extraordinary grace expanded my imagination, hopes and desires, surpassing anything I had ever thought possible for my life. For the first time, I truly was stepping into, onto the edge of my future, my destiny.

Doubt succumbed to hope, possibility, potential, and all the extraordinary dreams that would keep me stretching. The shackles and blinders of my previous existence fell away and I saw my true life, the true world, and the true destiny of humanity and of each soul.

I saw the lights of every soul on earth. I saw us all transcending our small narrow lives, lifting up into our true light, our true nature. I saw who we really are: We are large. We are a grand species. We are individuals filled with the ideal Self.

It was in this revelatory moment, the culmination of many days of out-of-body visions and transcendent travels, that I knew why I was in this life, this world, this body.

The very next breath I took was the first breath of my new life. I breathed for the first time with the fullness of Spirit, with the heart of a gentle and valiant soul, with the mind of a seer and a teacher of wisdom, to remind us all who we really are. For we have always been this grand Self. None of us has ever stopped being this grand Self.

In this moment of my first breath, I saw the wholeness of us all. I saw our glad hearts. I saw and felt the smiles and laughter of our true Nature. I felt the yearning of our hearts for release from pain and anguish. I felt the cries of our true beings for peace and sanity. I felt the pull of all souls in the world to find a way to be reminded of their inner light, to find a way to rekindle that connection, to find a way to remember and once again live from that place of our deep Self that is sacred and free of all regret.

In that moment, Spirit set itself upon me. Spirit opened my heart, my mind, my eyes, my ears, my tongue; giving me gifts of knowing, knowledge of the inner worlds, knowledge of our true Selves, knowledge and understanding of what we are and what we once again can be, knowledge of where we are evolving as a people, knowledge of how to help individuals remember.

In this hour of awakening to my true Self, my destiny came upon me as a cloak of surrender, no matter what the cost; a cloak of sanctity to give all that I am to help the people of this world find even a moment or a glimpse of what I *knew* in this single hour.

Since that day, I have had many hours, at times many months, of uninterrupted bliss and a continuous glow in the rapture of the Divine Presence breathing its force through me, that I may fulfill my purpose—which is to rekindle the *memory* of what we all are: divine beings.

That tremendous surging Vital Force still pushes me to transcend my everyday reality and to continue to reach out—because that is how we grow, that is how we each have made it this far, how we always have evolved and become more as a people and as individuals.

Awakened to my divine Nature, the fullness of Spirit flooded my being, flushed, purged, and nurtured my every thought and feeling to be a voice of the Divine, a hand of the Divine, to share with others whatever the Divine gives through me.

Graced by the splendid touch of God, thereafter transformed, I gave over my life wholly to be of service. That was the beginning of my life and the opening of my journey into my heart.

Vision 1

In a deep meditation, my oversoul spoke into my heart-mind and said, "My name is Samuel."

I saw him in a dream one quiet afternoon in Colorado during a short nap.

I looked up and this very handsome man in his forties walked toward me, dressed in a modest, brown monk's robe with a hood.

He came to me like a father. He came to me as a friend. He came without grandeur, but with a clear and steady gentleness.

And I knew: This is one called Oversoul. This one is the source of my being. This one is the purpose of my life, and I am to teach his message, given to each of us on Earth:

> "Be who you are, now, today. And fear not. For the true divinity, the wisdom, the strength, the guidance, is not an outer force or magic—but is you yourself.

> "*You* are the one who creates your life, your reality, your joy, your sorrow. *You* are the one with the power to change it.

> "The Divine Light is in all, without exception. You find that light when you pause in your busy life—and allow the breath of life to carry you into the womb of creation ... where you were born and always will exist.

> "You and all around you are a part of one Living Consciousness. And it is good. And so are you."

Vision 2

A delicate fragrance of rose potpourri filled my quiet room. I curled beneath my periwinkle-blue afghan and gazed out the bay window at the prisms of afternoon snow filling the crisp Colorado air, floating down softly and blanketing the earth white. The resonant dancing lights reached into my soul and embraced me.

Alive. I am. Forever.

In that moment, I could see beyond all boundaries, through all, and familiar thoughts streamed into my mind:

Be still. Be still and know that God is in you. Be still.

This mantra into my mind soothed me, calmed me, stroked away my fears.

Be still. Be still and know that God is in you. Be still.

Drowsiness overcame me and I drifted into a light nap, wherein I saw an iridescent figure. The familiar light-being took my hand, and warmth flowed through me. We lifted beyond this world to a very bright hall and stood before a large double door. It opened and we entered a lovely garden of flowers, with singing birds and flowing fountains.

The light-being departed and a tall, ageless, spiritual master walked toward me. His stride implied an inner strength born from much experience. Yet he came without grandeur, with a clear and steady gentleness. His brown hair and beard complemented his modest, brown priest's robe with a hood, of the ancient archetypal order of Melchizedek.

This handsome man, looking to be in his forties, came to me like a father. He came to me as a friend. His deep, brown eyes revealed a quiet and mellow nature.

"My name is Samuel," he said.

He took my hand and we strolled through the garden, as he explained that in one lifetime he had been known as the prophet

Samuel in the biblical Old Testament. After many lifetimes and inner explorations, he had grown beyond the boundaries of external reality and the struggles of human life. No longer bound to a body, he had ascended as his true Self into the timeless realms as one of the Unseen, now neither masculine nor feminine.

That was when he remembered he was an oversoul — *my* oversoul, the being from whom I first came to exist as an independent personality.

Until age thirty, I had journeyed throughout my life without consciously knowing of my oversoul's existence. Yet Samuel had guided me. His feelings had impressed me; and his thoughts had reached into my deepest self, embodying the soul presence into my life.

Samuel and I now came to a room of mirrors. "Why have you come?" he asked me.

"I want to know," I answered humbly.

"What do you want to know?"

"Whatever you will show me."

We walked through the room, looking at my own many reflections of different incarnations, and Samuel said of other Ascended Masters, angels, and himself, "We have little more knowing than you, but we have come far since physical life. Perhaps our insights and understanding will help you and your friends find an easier way."

"What can I do?" I asked.

"Give. That is all we ask. Let others know that life is not coming to any end. Let them know that they are each a divine aspect of the universal life force. Let them know that beings exist who respect and love them and offer support on request. Let them know all that we will tell you. Be our messenger. Let us teach through you."

We returned to the garden and, as Samuel departed, a tall slender woman with long midnight-black hair approached me. She gazed at me warmly with love and affection, and a reverence fell over me. Alexandra was the other half of me, my "twin flame," who also originally had come from the same oversoul; then she and I had decided to explore different kinds of reality as separate selves.

"My gift," she said, "is to give you all you have known and to lift you up. Prepare yourself, my friend. Join me now."

We walked and I listened and learned, transcending into expanded visions and hope.

"Indeed," said Alexandra, "there is always hope."

She and I planned the rest of my current life and I came to remember what I had known before about the realms of limitless thought.

We then traversed the universes and I brought back memories of these sojourns, which I share in this and many other books.

"Embrace all, be all," said Alexandra. "Know that your dreams are already fulfilled, even as you give yourself to them."

The Author

Futurist and global visionary Charol Messenger activated into Higher Self consciousness during a spontaneous awakening to cosmic consciousness and oversoul merge in 1975.[4]

Her books have received fifteen awards, including five international first and second place. Of these: First Place Winner *The New Humans* (Book 2 *"The New Humanity"* series) in the Soul-Bridge Book Awards of Europe 2017 in the category "Spiritual Awakening of Humanity," as well as Second Place International Book Excellence Award 2017 (sole Finalist) in Spirituality; plus three more Book Excellence Awards in 2016 include: First Place Winner *You 2.0* in Personal Growth, and Second Place Winner *Humanity 2.0* (Book 1 in *"The New Humanity"* series, fourth award) (sole Finalist) in Spirituality.

A *spiritual revealer* attuned to the undercurrent hum sweeping through humanity, Charol has helped over 65,000 individuals through her Higher Self books, blogs, classes, tweets and 20,500 spiritual soul readings as a Higher Self clairvoyant.

A certified lightworker (1990), certified clear channel of Ascended Masters and the Spiritual Hierarchy (1983), and messenger of her oversoul and Angels of Serendipity, in the Messenger books Charol is revealing Higher teachings on spiritual development, the new millennial spirituality, Higher Self integration for everyday life, understanding the inner voice, communicating with the angels, and humanity's spiritual transcendence and long-foretold evolutionary transformation — that is happening *right now*. Humanity is in *transcension*. We are in it, now.

Founder of the Books for Iraq charity (2004-05) and international newsletter *Global Citizen* (1987-88), Charol has a B.A. in English, philosophy, and world religions from the University of

---

4   For more on the oversoul, read *The Education of Oversoul Seven* by Jane Roberts, also my appendix "A Vision."

Colorado (1985). She is also an award-winning book editor. She lives in Colorado with her Yorkshire Terrier.

More About the Messenger

Charol Messenger spontaneously awakened to the universal consciousness at two a.m. November 2, 1975. As a result, she has the spiritual gifts of clearly hearing, discerning, and interpreting the language of the soul, the "language of light." She is a translator of esoteric knowledge and the *Living* Akashic Records into practical, everyday terms. All of the phases of her spiritual development have come upon her unbidden consciously and without any expectation. Each phase has been a part of her soul's plan for this lifetime.

Carrying the signature and blueprint of her oversoul—the biblical prophet Samuel—Charol "elected" to be born in July 1945, between VE Day and VJ Day at the end of World War II, to be a part of the upcoming transformative social changes on planet Earth.

In the fall of 1975, after a life-threatening situation over several weeks and shattering encounters with dark spirits, Charol faced the "dark night of the soul." Bombarded in her mind by images and tauntings by demons, she turned to prayer for the first time in many years and asked God for protection and guidance. At the culmination of this treacherous spiritual assault, she faced these forces of darkness, relentlessly standing in the light and refusing to give in.

It was during this fight for her soul that spiritual sight and gifts flooded to the surface of Charol's mind. She felt the presence of Archangel Michael *overlighting* her, saw a multitude of angels surrounding her amidst a heavenly glow and heard their chorus of song outside the Gates of Heaven. Amidst their expansive luminous light, new revelations about humanity's future came in waves to Charol, like a movie unfolding before her, scene by scene.

This spontaneous merge of Charol's oversoul consciousness into her personality took six-and-a-half years to fully integrate. Then for eleven days—from five days before through five days after March 5, 1982 (the day of a seven-planet alignment)—she was fully immersed in the exalted consciousness of her Higher Self.

Two months later, in May, Charol was wakened out of a deep sleep by a gentle inner voice speaking *into* her mind, the voice of an angel on her soul council. This was the beginning of a writing phase during which she received, through inner dictation, several books: on the spiritual path, the history and origin of the angels and how they help humanity, and our evolving human society. She was wakened out of a deep sleep each night by an inner prodding between two and four a.m. As she heard each word or phrase—in the dark, sitting up in bed—she repeated it into a cassette tape recorder. For twelve years, she transcribed, light edited, and integrated the information at a deep level of the self. She did not publish these works widely; she only shared excerpts with workshop participants as handouts and with close friends.

In 1994, Charol left a full-time clerical job in early April, yearning to renew a fuller connection with her spiritual Self. After seven weeks of very deep, two-hour meditations daily, one morning at the end of May during an especially deep meditation, she *lifted* to a place in higher consciousness she had never reached before (and didn't know she could, had not sought it or expected it).

On this day, Charol began a five-month period of 24/7 heightened clarity, during which she wrote five new books, writing from a new pristine place within her consciousness, the most pure place one can reach and bring back the insights to the world. Interestingly, she received the new inner-dictated materials in her own point of view as if she had sat down and written them, including anecdotes about her own life, which she had never before realized.

These five new books presented the same topics as those received twelve years before in 1982. But these new books came through flawlessly: on the angels in our everyday lives *(Wings of Light* and *Walking with Angels,* expanded second edition in production), living the spiritual path in physical life *(The Soul Path),* the origins and future of humanity *(The New Humanity,* which is also volume one in *Humanity 2.0),* and humanity's first incarnation *(The Memory,* expanded second edition in production). These books required minimal editing. Charol only added titles and subheadings and rearranged some chapters. All of the books are in second editions, 2018.

In 2012, Charol published *You 2.0: Living Your Infinite Self* (written in higher consciousness in 1989, needing only proofing). In 2017, she published *The New Humans: Second Genesis,* the first of many books collected from her blog, which was written in higher consciousness from the spring equinox of March 2011 through the spring equinox in 2017. Several other books are being collected from that blog, including: *Coded In Us, The Fourth Wave of Enlightened Humanity,* and *The New Millennial Spirituality.*

In 2019, *In Jesus' Words, Today: Humanity's Magnificent Future* (The New Jesus Chronicles, book 1) was published verbatim as received with zero editing. Charol only added section and chapter titles, initial caps and italics for higher divine meanings, and bullets and indenting for readers to hear Jesus' voice.

Published in 2020, *Your Awakening Attitude of Service: In Jesus' Words, Today, on the fifth level of consciousness* (The New Jesus Chronicles, book 2) was received in 1989.[5] It was edited in 2020; May through July, Jesus gave improvements in the simplicity of his message, because this book was intended for this year of the global pandemic.

---

5 Read appendix "This Book's Story" for why it took thirty years.

The Messenger Books

IN JESUS' WORDS, TODAY: Humanity's Magnificent Future – 2019 Kairos Award and two TV interviews with Preach the Word Worldwide Network.

THE NEW HUMANS: Second Genesis – First Place Winner in Soul Bridge Book Awards of Europe 2017 in "The Spiritual Awakening of Humanity;" and Second Place Book Excellence Award 2017 (Canada) in Body-Mind-Spirit. 2018 2nd Ed.

HUMANITY 2.0: The New Humanity – Five awards include: 2019 honorary Shining Stars Crystal Award plus TV interview with Preach the Word Worldwide Network. Second Place international Book Excellence Award 2016 in Spirituality. 2018 2nd Ed.

YOU 2.0: Living Your Infinite Self – First Place Winner in Book Excellence Awards 2016 in Personal Growth. 2018 2nd Ed.

THE SOUL PATH – National Finalist 2015 USA Best Books in General Spirituality. 2018 3rd Ed.

INTUITION FOR EVERY DAY, a spirituality everyday workbook – National Finalist 2015 USA Best Books New Age Nonfiction. 2018 2nd Ed.

WINGS OF LIGHT: The Four Angels Who Guide You – National Finalist CIPA EVVY 2012 in Spirituality. 2018 2nd Ed.

THE POWER OF COURAGE: An Uplifting Saga of Moving Beyond Abuse — Second Place Winner 2016 international Book Excellence Awards in New Nonfiction; and National Finalist 2015 USA Best Books in Women's Issues. (currently adding a present-day personal Introduction).

I'M DANCING AS FAST AS I CAN – National Finalist 2005 USA Best Books, a memoir comprised of narrative poetic vignettes.

Charol is a certified clear channel of Ascended Masters through The Tibetan Foundation (1983) and a certified lightworker from Linda Schiller-Hanna (1990), founder of the Books for Iraq charity and publisher of the 1987-88 international newsletter *Global Citizen*. She has a B.A. in English, philosophy, and world religions from the University of Colorado, 1985.

Recommended Movies, Books, Audio, Video

I highly recommend:

2017 movie, *A Dog's Purpose,* based on the book *A Dog's Way Home* by w. Bruce Cameron

2016 movie, Marvel's *Dr. Strange*

2017 book, *Gifts from the Edge,* Claudia Watts Edge, a personal favorite, true insights and visions of life beyond death

In addition:

Hands of Light, Barbara Ann Brennan

Vision, Ken Carey, Harper San Francisco

Mastery Through Accomplishment, Hazrat Inayat Khan

Freedom in Exile: The Autobiography of the Dalai Lama

Surfing the Himalayas, Frederick Lenz

The Seat of the Soul, Gary Zukav

Living with Joy, Sanaya Roman

The Possible Human, Jean Houston

The Cultural Creatives, Paul H. Ray

Initiation, Elizabeth Haich

The Sacred Journey: You and Your Higher Self, Lazaris

Space-Time and Beyond, Toben and Wolf

Illusions, Jonathan Livingston Seagull, Richard Bach

The Education of Oversoul Seven, Jane Roberts

Psychic Self-Defense and Well-Being, Melita Denning and Osborne Phillips

The Impersonal Life, DeVorss & Co., Publishers

Life and Teaching of the Masters of the Far East, Baird T. Spalding

The Celestine Prophecy, James Redfield, Warner Books

"Getting in the Gap," Wayne Dyer

Pathways to Mastership, audio set, Jonathan Parker; Gateways Institute

"Chakra Balancing and Energizing" audio, Dick Sutphen

Joseph Campbell videos on mythology

I have not read the following books, so as not to influence my own writings, but I recommend them based on their topics, for a broad view of what visionaries are sharing.

The Third Millennium, Ken Carey, Harper San Francisco

The Power of Now, The New Earth, Eckhart Tolle

Bashar: Blueprint for change, Darryl Anka, New Solutions Publishing

New Cells, New Bodies, New Life! Virginia Essene, S.E.E. Publishing

You Are Becoming a Galactic Human, Virginia Essene and Sheldon Nidle

My eternal love for my mom DJ who always believed in me. I dedicate all of these books to her, gentle and sweet spirit.

Also my love to my sister Jo, for our friendship.

My eternal gratitude to my dearest friend Barbara Munson for her irreplaceable support and friendship. She keeps me motivated and encouraged, and she is always there for me when I need another pair of eyes on final details.

My deep gratitude to Keith Klein and Mary Ann Klein. Their limitless grace allows me to do this fulfilling work with contentment.

My great appreciation to the thousands who have participated in the teachings given in these books; especially the *many* good souls who have gifted me throughout my life in innumerable ways, including: John Brennan, Marja Pheasant, JoAnn Goldsmith, Matthew Patterson, John Cloonan, and Ray Alcott.

Especially, I owe everything to the divine beings who guide me: my oversoul and soul council, the Angels of Serendipity, and the All Mind from whom all wisdom flows.

Wakened at 3:00 a.m. by the inner guide,
who whispered:

"Sometimes you just have to believe."